DIABETIC AIR FRYER COOKBOOK

1200 Days of Delicious and Healthy Recipes to Take Care of Yourself While Still Enjoying the Food You Love

Jennifer May Johnson

INTRODUCTION	6
LIVING WITH DIABETES	6
RECIPES	16
Breakfast recipes	17
Scrambled Eggs	17
Cauliflower Avocado Toast	18
Air Fryer Hard-Boiled Eggs	19
Pancake Cake	19
Stuffed Poblanos	20
Spaghetti Squash Fritters	20
Sausage and Cheese Balls	21
Cheesy Cauliflower Hash Browns	22
Vegetarian Recipes	24
BBQ "Pulled" Mushrooms	24
Broccoli Crust Pizza	25
Caprese Eggplant Stacks	25
Zucchini Cauliflower Fritters	26
Air Fryer Green Beans	27
Air Fryer Brussel Sprouts	27
Quiche-Stuffed Peppers	29
Whole Roasted Lemon Cauliflower	29
Roasted Broccoli Salad	30
Cheesy Zoodle Bake	31
Roasted Veggie Bowl	32
Veggie Quesadilla	32
Portobello Mini Pizzas	33
Three-Cheese Zucchini Boats	34
Italian Baked Egg and Veggies	35
Crustless Spinach Cheese Pie	36
Greek Stuffed Eggplant	37
Loaded Cauliflower Steak	38
Spicy Parmesan Artichokes	39
Basic Spaghetti Squash	39
Cheesy Cauliflower Pizza Crust	40
FISH / SEAFOOD AIRFRYER RECIPES	41
Salmon Patties	41
Spicy Salmon Jerky	42
Air Fryer Salmon Fillets	43
Basil Parmesan Crusted Salmon	43
Air Fryer Lobster Tails with Lemon-Garlic Butter	44
Air Fryer Shrimp and Polenta	45
Air Fryer Lemon Pepper Shrimp	46
Cilantro Lime Baked Salmon	47
Buttery Cod	47
Shrimp Kebabs	48
Sesame-Crusted Tuna Steak	49
Crab Cakes	49
Fish Taco Bowl With Jalapeño Slaw	50
Fried Tuna Salad Bites	51
Tuna Zoodle Casserole	51

Crab Legs	52
Foil-Packet Salmon	53
Coconut Shrimp	53
Lemon Garlic Shrimp	54
Almond Pesto Salmon	55
Crispy Fish Sticks	55
Poultry Recipes	56
Spinach and Feta-Stuffed Chicken Breast	56
Air Fryer Low Carb Nashville Hot Chicken Sandwich	57
Cilantro Lime Chicken Thighs	58
Air Fryer Buttermilk Fried Chicken	59
Crispy Buffalo Chicken Tenders	60
Italian Chicken Thighs	61
Air Fryer Buffalo Chicken Meatballs	62
Almond-Crusted Chicken	63
Honey Balsamic Air Fryer Chicken Thighs	64
Chicken Pizza Crust	65
Blackened Cajun Chicken Tenders	65
Lemon Pepper Drumsticks	66
Jalapeño Popper Hasselback Chicken	67
Healthy Air Fryer Chicken and Veggies	68
Teriyaki Wings	69
Bang Bang Chicken	70
Chicken Cordon Bleu Casserole	71
Fajita-Stuffed Chicken Breast	71
Broccoli Cheddar Chicken Fritters	72
Chicken Enchiladas	73
Pepperoni and Chicken Pizza Bake	74
Chicken Patties	74
Chicken, Spinach, and Feta Bites	75
Greek Chicken Stir-Fry	76
Beef Recipes	77
Air Fryer Steak Bites and Mushrooms	77
Crispy Brats	78
Taco-Stuffed Peppers	78
Beef Burrito Bowl	79
Classic Mini Meatloaf	80
Chorizo and Beef Burger	81
Bacon Cheeseburger Casserole	82
Peppercorn-Crusted Beef Tenderloin	83
Easy Lasagna Casserole	83
Ground Beef Taco Rolls	84
Air Fryer Steak With Garlic-Herb Butter	85
Air-Fried Pizza Burgers	86
Oversized BBQ Meatballs	87
Empanadas	88
Reverse Seared Ribeye	89
Pub-Style Burger	90
Fajita Flank Steak Rolls	91
Air Fryer Juicy Steak Bites	92

Air Fryer Beef and Bean Chimichangas	93
Meatloaf Slider Wraps	94
Pork Recipes	95
Pork Rind Nachos	95
Crispy Pork Chop Salad	96
Breaded Pork Chops	97
Easy Juicy Pork Chops	97
Pulled Pork	98
Italian Stuffed Bell Peppers	99
Air Fryer Pork Chops and Broccoli	100
Keto Air Fryer Pork Belly Bites	101
Lemon and Honey Pork Tenderloin	102
Pork Burgers With Red Cabbage Slaw	102
Pork Taquitos in Air Fryer	103
Lamb Recipes	104
Garlic Sauce and Lamb Chops	104
Greek Lamb Pita Pockets	105
Rosemary Lamb Chops	106
Spicy Lamb Sirloin Steak	107
Air Fryer Lamb Chops	108
Herbed Lamb Chops	109
Appetizer Recipes	110
Mini Sweet Pepper Poppers	110
Ranch Roasted Almonds	111
Low Carb Lemon Blueberry Muffins (Air Fryer)	112
Mozzarella Pizza Crust	113
Air Fryer Stuffed Mushrooms	114
Bacon-Wrapped Jalapeño Poppers	115
Prosciutto-Wrapped Parmesan Asparagus	116
Bacon-Wrapped Onion Rings	117
Spicy Spinach Artichoke Dip	118
Garlic Cheese Bread	119
Beef Jerky	120
Mozzarella-Stuffed Meatballs	121
Spicy Buffalo Chicken Dip	122
Crustless Three-Meat Pizza	123
Garlic Tomatoes	123
Side dishes	124
Roasted Garlic	124
Veggie Quesadilla	125
Kale Chips	126
Zucchini Parmesan Chips	126
Fried Pickles	127
Roasted Eggplant	128
Avocado Fries	128
Coconut Flour Cheesy Garlic Biscuits	129
Cilantro Lime Roasted Cauliflower	130
Desserts	131
Coconut Flour Mug Cake	131
Almond Butter Cookie Balls	132

Vanilla Pound Cake	133
Pecan Brownies	134
Blackberry Crisp	135
Pumpkin Spice Pecans	136
Toasted Coconut Flakes	136
Pan Peanut Butter Cookies	137
Mini Cheesecake	138

INTRODUCTION

Diabetes is a disorder in which the body cannot regulate the amount of glucose in the bloodstream efficiently, causing a buildup of glucose (also called sugar) in the blood. Because cells require glucose for fuel, the lack of insulin, or the body's inability to use insulin properly, results in the breakdown of fatty tissue. This breakdown produces acids called ketones, which build up in the blood, causing ketoacidosis. As ketones build up in the body, they become stronger acids, further destroying body tissues.

Diabetes is a serious illness that affects 1 out of every 10 adults in the United States. 1.8 million new cases occur each year, and it is the 7th leading cause of death in the United States. It can lead to blindness, kidney failure, heart disease, and stroke. It is caused by a hormone called insulin. Insulin is a hormone that helps the body store and uses glucose (a form of sugar). When there is too little or no insulin or the body does not use it correctly, glucose stays in the blood. This can cause high blood sugar levels and damage to the eyes, kidneys, nerves, and heart.

Diabetics should eat a low-fat, high-fiber diet to help keep blood sugar levels under control. It is important to check with your doctor before making any changes to your normal routine. Eating several small meals and snacks throughout the day, instead of two or three large meals, helps to keep blood sugar levels stable. Exercise is also important in the management of diabetes, but you should check with your doctor before starting any type of exercise program.

The most common early symptoms of diabetes are frequent urination and extreme thirst. One of the most important ways to prevent diabetes is to keep your weight in a healthy range. The best way to lower your risk of diabetes and maintain your weight is to eat a healthy diet and exercise. If you are overweight, losing even 5 to 10 percent of your body weight can have a big impact on your health. You can do this by eating less and by exercising more. You should follow a diet that is high in fiber, low in fat, and low in cholesterol. And you should exercise at least 30 minutes on most days of the week.

LIVING WITH DIABETES

Living With Diabetes is a daily challenge for many diabetics and their families. The encouraging news is that most people with diabetes can manage their disease, and you can control your diabetes. It might be difficult to keep your blood sugar levels within the range prescribed by your doctor. This is because several things can cause your blood sugar levels to fluctuate, often unexpectedly. The following are some of the elements that might influence your blood sugar levels.

Food

Healthy nutrition is an essential component of having a healthy lifestyle, whether you have diabetes or not. However, if you have diabetes, you must understand how meals impact your blood sugar levels. It is not just the sort of food you consume, but also how much you eat and how you combine different types of food.
What to do:
- **Study carbohydrate counting and portion sizes.** Learning how to measure carbs is an important part of many diabetes control strategies. Carbohydrates have the greatest influence on blood sugar levels. It is critical for persons using mealtime insulin to understand the number of carbs in their diet so that they receive the correct insulin dose. Study the proper portion size for each meal type. Write down

quantities for things you consume frequently to make meal planning easier. To guarantee adequate portion size and an exact carbohydrate count, use measuring cups or a scale.

- **Make sure that every meal is well-balanced.** Plan your meals to include a variety of grains, fruits and vegetables, proteins, and fats as much as possible. Pay attention to the carbs you consume. Some carbs are better for you than others, such as fruits, vegetables, and whole grains. These meals are low in carbs and high in fiber, which helps maintain blood sugar levels constant. Consult your doctor, nurse, or nutritionist about the optimal dietary choices and the proper food type balance.
- **Plan your meals and meds.** Too little food concerning your diabetes treatments, particularly insulin, might result in dangerously low blood sugar levels (hypoglycemia). Too much eating may cause your blood sugar level to skyrocket (hyperglycemia). Discuss how to effectively coordinate meal and medication schedules with your diabetic health care team.
- **Avoid drinks with added sugar.** Sugar-sweetened drinks are heavy in calories and low in nutrients. If you have diabetes, you should avoid these drinks since they cause blood sugar to spike fast. The only exception is if you have a low blood sugar level. Sugar-sweetened beverages, such as soda, juice, and sports drinks, can be used to fast raise blood sugar levels that are too low.

Exercise

Physical activity is another critical component of your diabetes control strategy. Your muscles utilize sugar (glucose) for energy while you work out. Regular physical exercise also aids your body's usage of insulin.

These elements work together to reduce your blood sugar level. The longer the impact lasts, the more rigorous your workout. However, even simple tasks like cleaning, gardening, or standing for long periods might help your blood sugar.

What to do:

- **Consult your doctor about an exercise program.** Consult your doctor about the best sort of exercise for you. In general, most individuals should engage in at least 150 minutes of moderate aerobic exercise every week. On most days of the week, aim for 30 minutes of moderate aerobic activity. If you've been inactive for a long period, your doctor may want to assess your general health before making a recommendation. He or she can advise on the best combination of aerobic and muscle-strengthening activities.
- **Maintain a regular workout routine.** Consult your doctor about the optimal time of day to exercise so that your workout program coincides with your food and prescription routines.
- **Understand your numbers.** Before you begin exercising, consult with your doctor about what blood sugar levels are appropriate for you.
- **Examine your blood sugar levels.** Check your blood sugar levels before, during, and after exercise, especially if you take insulin or blood-sugar-lowering drugs. Exercise can drop your blood sugar levels even up to a day later, especially if you're doing it for the first time or at a higher intensity. Be mindful of symptoms of low blood sugar, such as shakiness, weakness, fatigue, hunger, lightheadedness, irritability, anxiety, or confusion. If you use insulin and your blood sugar level is less than 90 milligrams per deciliter (mg/dL) or 5.0 millimoles per liter (mmol/L), have a modest snack before you begin exercising to avoid hypoglycemia.
- **Keep hydrated.** While exercising, drink lots of water or other fluids since dehydration might alter blood sugar levels.
- **Prepare yourself.** Carry a small snack or glucose tablet with you when exercising in case your blood sugar gets too low. Wear a medical identification bracelet at all times.
- **As required, modify your diabetes treatment strategy.** If you use insulin, you may need to lower your insulin dose before exercising and closely check your blood sugar for many hours after strenuous

exercise since delayed hypoglycemia can occur. Your doctor can advise you on proper drug modifications. If you've increased your workout habit, you may need to modify your therapy.

Medication

When diet and exercise are insufficient for treating diabetes, insulin and other diabetic medicines are used to reduce blood sugar levels. The success of these drugs, however, is dependent on the time and size of the dose. Medications used for diseases other than diabetes might potentially have an impact on your blood sugar levels.

What to do:

- **Insulin should be stored correctly.** Insulin that has been incorrectly kept or has passed its expiry date may no longer be effective. Insulin is very sensitive to temperature fluctuations.
- **Inform your doctor about any issues.** If your diabetes drugs cause your blood sugar to dip too low or rise too high regularly, the dosage or timing may need to be modified.
- **Be wary of new drugs.** If you are thinking about taking an over-the-counter medicine or if your doctor prescribes a new medication to address another illness, such as high blood pressure or high cholesterol, ask your doctor or pharmacist if the medication will impact your blood sugar levels.
- **A different drug may be prescribed in some cases.** Always with your doctor before starting any new over-the-counter medicine so you understand how it will affect your blood sugar level.

Illness

When you're unwell, your body creates stress hormones that aid in the battle against the sickness, but they can also elevate your blood sugar level. Diabetes control may also be complicated by changes in your appetite and daily activities.

What to do:

- **Make a plan.** Create a sick-day strategy with your healthcare team. Include instructions on what drugs to take, how frequently to check your blood sugar and urine ketone levels, how to alter your medication dosages, and when to contact your doctor.
- **Take your diabetic medication as usual.** Contact your doctor if you are unable to eat due to nausea or vomiting. Because of the risk of hypoglycemia, you may need to alter your insulin dose or temporarily reduce or discontinue short-acting insulin or diabetic medication. Do not, however, discontinue your long-acting insulin. It is critical to test your blood glucose often during sickness, and your doctor may also urge you to check your urine for the presence of ketones.
- **Maintain your diabetic food plan.** Eating normally will help you regulate your blood sugar levels if you can. Keep stomach-friendly items on your hands, such as gelatin, crackers, soups, and applesauce. To keep hydrated, drink plenty of water or other non-calorie-containing drinks, such as tea. If you use insulin, you may need to drink sugar-sweetened drinks, such as juice or a sports drink, to prevent your blood sugar from dipping too low.

Alcohol

To compensate for declining blood sugar levels, the liver generally releases stored sugar. However, if your liver is busy metabolizing alcohol, your blood sugar level may not receive the necessary boost from your liver. Alcohol can cause low blood sugar levels quickly after consumption and for up to 24 hours thereafter.
What to do:

- **Obtain permission from your doctor to consume alcohol.** Diabetes issues such as nerve damage and eye disease might be exacerbated by alcohol. However, if your diabetes is under control and your doctor approves, an occasional alcoholic beverage is OK. Moderate alcohol intake is defined as one drink per day for women of any age and men over the age of 65, and two drinks per day for males under the age of 65. A 12-ounce beer, 5 ounces of wine, or 1.5 ounces of distilled liquor equals one drink.
- **Never consume alcoholic drinks on an empty stomach.** To avoid low blood sugar, eat before drinking or drink with a meal if you take insulin or other diabetic treatments.
- **Choose your drinks with caution.** Light beer and dry wines contain fewer calories and carbs than other alcoholic beverages. Sugar-free mixers, such as diet soda, diet tonic, club soda, or seltzer, will not boost your blood sugar.
- **Count your calories.** Include the calories from any alcohol you consume in your daily calorie total. Inquire with your doctor or a nutritionist about including calories and carbs from alcoholic beverages into your diet plan.
- **Before going to bed, check your blood sugar level.** Check your blood sugar level before going to bed since alcohol can drop blood sugar levels long after you've had your last drink. If your blood sugar isn't between 100 and 140 mg/dL (5.6 and 7.8 mmol/L), have a snack before bed to compensate for a decline.

DIFFERENT TYPES OF DIABETES

- Type 1 diabetes: This is an autoimmune condition, which means your body assaults itself. The insulin-producing cells in your pancreas are damaged in this situation. Type 1 diabetes affects up to 10% of all diabetics. It is most commonly diagnosed in children and young adults (but can develop at any age). Diabetes was once classified as "juvenile" diabetes. People with Type 1 diabetes must take insulin daily. This is why it's sometimes referred to as insulin-dependent diabetes.
- Type 2 diabetes: This kind occurs when your body either does not produce enough insulin or when your cells do not respond appropriately to insulin. This is the most prevalent kind of diabetes. Type 2 diabetes affects up to 95% of diabetics. It commonly affects persons in their forties and fifties. Type 2 diabetes is also known as adult-onset diabetes and insulin-resistant diabetes. It may have been referred to as "having a touch of sweetness" by your parents or grandparents.
- Prediabetes: This is the stage before Type 2 diabetes. Your blood glucose levels are greater than usual, but not high enough to be identified as having Type 2 diabetes.
- Gestational diabetes: Some women develop this kind throughout their pregnancy. Gestational diabetes normally disappears after pregnancy. However, if you have gestational diabetes, you are more likely to acquire Type 2 diabetes later in life.

Diabetes kinds that are less prevalent include:
- Monogenic diabetes syndromes: These are uncommon hereditary types of diabetes that account for up to 4% of all cases. Neonatal diabetes and young-onset diabetes are two examples.
- Diabetes caused by cystic fibrosis: This is a kind of diabetes that only affects persons who have this condition.
- Drug or chemical-induced diabetes: Examples of this kind occur during organ transplantation, HIV/AIDS therapy, or are related to the use of glucocorticoid steroids.

HEALTHY EATING TIPS FOR DIABETES

1. Consume three meals every day, including breakfast.
2. Make an effort not to skip meals.
3. Meals should be spaced 4 to 6 hours apart.
4. Breakfast, lunch, and dinner should all be around the same size.
5. Avoid extremely large or extremely tiny meals.
6. At each meal, consume one piece of fresh fruit.
7. Limit yourself to 1/2 cup of juice every day.
8. Limit your consumption of high-fat meals, such as deep-fried or fried dishes.
9. Limit meat servings to the size of your palm and opt for fish or skinless chicken more regularly.
10. Keep an eye out for extra fats. Select low-fat or fat-free dressings and spreads.

FOODS AND DRINKS TO LIMITS

Foods and drinks to reduce include:
- foods rich in saturated fat and trans fat
- foods high in salt, also known as sodium
- sweets, such as baked goods, candy, and ice cream
- drinks with added sugars, such as juice, regular soda, and regular sports or energy drinks

Drink water instead of sugary drinks. Use a sugar replacement in your coffee or tea.

If you drink alcohol, limit yourself to one drink per day for women and two drinks per day for men. Alcohol might cause your blood glucose level to drop too low if you use insulin or diabetic medications that enhance the amount of insulin your body produces. This is particularly true if you haven't eaten in a long time. When drinking alcohol, it is recommended to have some food.

BEST DIETS WHEN YOU HAVE DIABETES

Check All the Boxes
The appropriate diet can help you regulate your blood sugar, lose weight, and feel better. Several well-known and popular eating programs may provide you with the roadmap to accomplish so. You'll want to find something that you can stick to, with meals you enjoy.

Start With the Basics
Keep an eye on your calorie intake and portion sizes. Reduce your consumption of fried meals, sweets, sugary drinks, and anything salty or greasy. Instead, load up on vegetables, whole grains, lean protein, low-fat dairy, fruit, and healthy fats. To keep your blood sugar levels stable, you may need to eat every several hours. Your doctor or diabetes educator can assist you in fine-tuning a diet to suit your needs.

Low-Carb
Because you have diabetes, you do not have to give up carbs. If you wish to attempt a diet that limits them, such as Atkins or South Beach, see your doctor first. The evidence on the advantages of low-carbohydrate diets for type 2 diabetes is still divided. However, according to a review authored by 25 renowned specialists, this eating pattern should be the first step in controlling the condition since it may "reliably lower high blood glucose."

Mediterranean Diet

This heart-healthy diet incorporates a variety of fruits and vegetables as well as fish, poultry, nuts, olive oil, legumes, and whole grains. Red meat, butter, and salt are things you won't consume very often. According to research, the diet can help maintain blood sugar levels under control. Wine can be consumed with meals, but the American Diabetes Association recommends no more than one glass per day for women and two for men.

DASH

Many individuals endorse this blood-pressure-lowering eating plan because it emphasizes fruits, vegetables, low-fat dairy, healthy grains, lean meats, fish, nuts, and beans. (It also allows for certain sweets.) You should consume them in moderation.) According to a 2011 research, it can enhance insulin sensitivity when used with a weight loss program that includes exercise.

The Zone Diet

Its purpose is to maintain steady blood sugar levels. Meals contain 40% carbohydrates, 30% protein, and 30% fat. The glycemic index ranks carbohydrates as beneficial or unfavorable. Chicken and barley will be available, but not potatoes or egg yolks. According to a 2015 study, it has a favorable influence on glycemic management and waist size, therefore it might be an excellent choice. Consult your doctor about it.

Weight Watchers

You are given a certain number of points to "spend" while eating. Most veggies have 0 points, so you may eat as much as you want of them, but fast meals and sweets have high point values. According to studies, it is effective. In addition, the firm provides a program for persons with type 2 diabetes that includes fitness guidance and assistance from a counselor who is knowledgeable about the disease's treatment.

Prepackaged Diet Meals

There is a vast range of ready-made meals available, whether you have them delivered to your home or pick them up at a grocery shop. Be cautious: their ingredient lists can be lengthy, and they aren't necessarily diabetic-friendly. Some companies, like Nutrisystem and Jenny Craig, do provide diabetes-specific meals. Consult your doctor to help you narrow down your options.

Paleo

The concept behind this fashionable diet is to eat as early humans did before modern agriculture when we were hunter-gatherers. This includes no dairy, refined sugar, cereals, or legumes as well as no processed vegetable oils such as soybean or canola oil. Fruits and vegetables, lean meats (ideally grass-fed), seafood, nuts, and seeds are all acceptable. Small studies indicate that this dietary pattern can help with blood sugar and diabetes.

Gluten-Free

Gluten is a protein that is present in grains such as wheat, rye, and barley. People with digestive issues, such as celiac disease, should avoid it. Going gluten-free is widely believed to help you reduce weight, improve digestion, and increase energy. However, research does not support these statements. Furthermore, gluten may be found in anything from salad dressing to vitamins. This diet is not necessary unless your doctor recommends it.

Vegetarian and Vegan

It is possible to eat healthily by limiting or avoiding animal products such as chicken, fish, and yogurt. Simply eat plenty of fresh veggies and other complete meals instead of binging on vegetarian "chicken" nuggets from a box. According to research, people who follow a plant-based diet obtain more fiber and consume fewer calories and fat than nonvegetarians. However, speak with a qualified nutritionist to verify that your vegan or vegetarian diet fits your nutritional demands.

Raw Foods
This diet adherents think that excessive heating temperatures destroy important nutrients in food. They consume a lot of fresh vegetables, seeds, and nuts, and they cook using equipment like blenders and dehydrators. Although this type of eating is likely to help you lose weight, there is no proof that it improves diabetic symptoms. The basic line is that there are healthier, more effective diets available.

Alkaline Diet
The reasoning behind this diet is that items like bread, pork, and sugar increase acidity in the body, which can cause long-term problems. Vegetables and seeds, on the other hand, can change your body chemistry and make it more alkaline, allowing you to lose weight and stay healthy. There is little evidence to back up these claims, so skip this one for the time being.

DIABETES MEAL PLANNING

A meal plan serves as a guide for when, what, and how much to eat to acquire the nourishment you require while maintaining your blood sugar levels within your goal range. A smart meal plan will take your objectives, tastes, and lifestyle into account, as well as any medications you're taking.

A decent food plan will also include:
- Increase your intake of nonstarchy veggies including broccoli, spinach, and green beans.
- Reduce the amount of added sugars and refined carbohydrates in your diet, such as white bread, rice, and pasta with less than 2 grams of fiber.
- external icon
- per serving.
- Choose whole foods over heavily processed meals.
- external icon
- as much as possible.

Carbohydrates in diet cause blood sugar levels to rise. The rate at which carbohydrates raise your blood sugar depends on the food and what you consume with it. Drinking fruit juice, for example, boosts blood sugar quicker than eating whole fruit. Eating carbohydrates with protein, fat, or fiber decreases the rate at which your blood sugar increases.

To avoid high or low blood sugar levels, arrange for regular, balanced meals. Eating roughly the same quantity of carbohydrates at each meal can be beneficial. Counting carbohydrates and utilizing the plate method are two typical strategies that might help with meal planning.

Carbohydrate counting
Carbohydrate counting entails keeping note of how many carbs you consume each day. Carbohydrates impact your blood glucose level more than other foods since they convert to glucose in your body. Carbohydrate counting can assist you in controlling your blood glucose levels. If you need insulin, tracking carbs might help you figure out how much to take.

Carbohydrate counting is a meal planning technique for diabetics who use insulin, however, not all diabetics must count carbs. Your health care team can assist you in developing a personalized dietary plan that will best fit your needs.

Carbohydrate content in foods is measured in grams. You'll need a scale to count carbohydrate grams in your diet.

- Learn which foods contain carbs.
- Check the Nutrition Facts food label or learn to estimate the number of carbohydrates in the meals you consume.
- Add the carbohydrate grams from each food you eat to determine your total for the day and each meal.

Most of the carbs are found in grains, fruits, milk, and sweets. Limit carbohydrate sources with added sugars or refined grains, such as white bread and white rice. Consume carbs from fruits and vegetables, whole grains, legumes, and low-fat or nonfat milk instead.

Plate method

The plate approach allows you to better regulate your portion amounts. You are not required to count calories. The plate technique indicates how much of each food group you should consume. This strategy is most effective for lunch and dinner.

Make use of a 9-inch plate. Half of the dish should be nonstarchy vegetables; one-fourth should be meat or other protein, and the remaining one-fourth should be a grain or other starch. Starchy veggies such as maize and peas are examples of starches. You may also have a small bowl of fruit or a piece of fruit and a tiny glass of milk as part of your meal plan.

Small snacks between meals may also be included in your regular eating regimen.

Portion sizes

To determine the size of a piece, utilize ordinary items or your hand:
- 1 serving of meat or poultry is approximately the size of your palm or a deck of cards.
- 1 3-ounce plate of fish is equivalent to a checkbook.
- Six dice of cheese are one serving.
- A rounded handful or a tennis ball of cooked rice or pasta equals 1/2 cup.
- 1 dish of pancakes or waffles equals 1 DVD.
- A ping-pong ball is 2 teaspoons of peanut butter.

ADVANTAGES OF DIABETES DIETS

Blood Sugar Control

The main objective of diabetes management is to get your blood sugar levels as near to normal as possible. Your doctor can help you figure out your blood sugar targets, but in general, they should be between 90 and 130 milligrams per deciliter before meals and fewer than 180 milligrams per deciliter two hours after. Your blood sugar levels are affected by the carbs you consume. A diabetic diet allows you to limit the amount of carbs you consume each day and at each meal for improved blood sugar control. Controlling your blood sugar levels may lower your risk of diabetic complications.

Weight Management

In general, the diabetic diet is beneficial. The diet encourages you to eat items from all food categories, with an emphasis on fruits and vegetables, healthy grains, lean protein sources, and low-fat dairy. The diet also promotes portion management and eating meals on a regular basis. These healthy diet guidelines are similar to those recommended to those who desire to reduce weight. If you have diabetes and are overweight or obese, decreasing as little as 10 pounds will help improve your blood sugar.

HEALTHY LIVING AND AIR-FRYING

In terms of roasting and baking, an air fryer is similar to an oven. Still, the heating components are only on top and are assisted by a powerful, huge fan, resulting in beautifully crisp food in no time. Instead of a vat of boiling oil, the air fryer uses rotating heated air to conveniently and consistently cook food. This is placed in a metal basket (mesh) or a rack to enable hot air to circulate uniformly over the food, providing the same light golden, crispy crunch as frying in oil. It's a simple air fryer that cooks food faster than frying and cleans up easily. You may make a variety of nutritious meals such as fruits, meat, fish, chicken, and more, as well as healthier versions of your favorite fried dishes such as chips, onion rings, or French fries.

HOW AN AIR FRYER WORKS

The air fryer is a convection oven with a hotter countertop. Its compact size allows for significantly faster cooking. A heating device and a fan are kept at the gadget's top. Hot air circulates through and around the food in a basket-style fryer. This rapid circulation, like deep frying, crisps the food. It's also quite easy to clean, and most systems have dishwasher-safe components.

COOKING WITH AN AIR FRYER

Once you understand how to use an air fryer, you may use it to heat frozen items or cook fresh dishes such as poultry, salmon, other shellfish, pork chops, and veggies. Most meats do not require extra oil since they are still moist:

- Season with salt and your preferred herbs and spices.
- Make careful to use dry spices; less moisture leads to crisper results.
- Wait until the last few minutes of cooking to baste the steak with any sauce or barbecue sauce.
- Browning is required for lean meat cuts or things with little or no fat, and crisping requires a spray of oil. Before cooking, clean the pork chops and boneless chicken breasts and lightly oil them. Because of its greater smoke point, vegetable oil or canola oil is often selected, ensuring that it can withstand the severe heat of an air fryer.
- Vegetables are frequently coated with oil before being air-fried. Season them with salt. Use less than you normally would. The crunchy parts that are air-fried provide a lot of taste. Fried baby potato halves, broccoli florets, and Brussels sprouts are all delicious. They're so clean. Sweet potatoes, butternut squash, peppers, and green beans all tend to get sweeter as they cook.

TIP FOR COOKING IN AN AIR FRYER FOR BEGINNERS

Shake the basket: Before cooking, open the fryer and shake the food about in the tray, compressing smaller items like French fries and chips. To improve performance, toss them every 5 to 10 minutes.
Do not overcrowd the basket: Allowing enough of space for meals so that air can flow properly is what produces crispy results.
Spray the food with oil: Check that the food does not stick to the bowl. Brush meals lightly with cooking spray.

Keep the food dry: Before frying, ensure sure the food is completely dry to avoid splattering and excessive smoke (even if you marinate it). Similarly, while producing high-fat dishes like chicken wings, make sure to frequently clean the oil from the bottom of the machine.

Other uses for air frying include: The air fryer is ideal for a variety of healthy cooking methods, including grilling, baking, and roasting.

Few other tips are:
- To ensure even cooking, divide the meal into equal portions.
- Distribute the food in the air fryer basket in a single thin, uniform layer. Food may become less crispy if the basket is overcrowded.
- A small amount of oil would produce the same light, golden, crispy crust as frying. Apply a thin, uniform coating of oil to the meal with cooking spray or an oil mister.
- The air fryer is useful for reheating dishes, especially those with a crispy exterior.

BENEFITS OF USING AN AIR FRYER

- Easy cleanup
- Low-fat meals
- Less oil is needed
- Cooks food evenly
- Weight loss
- Reduced cancer risk
- Diabetes management
- Improved memory
- Improved gut health

RECIPES

Breakfast recipes

Scrambled Eggs

Prep Time: 5 minutes
Cook Time: 15 minutes
Serves 2

Ingredients
- 4 large eggs
- 2 tablespoons unsalted butter, melted
- 1/2 cup shredded sharp Cheddar cheese

Preparation
1. Whisk eggs after cracking them into a 2-cup round baking dish. Put the dish in the basket of the air fryer.
2. Set the timer for 10 minutes and raise the temperature to 400°F.
3. Stir the eggs and incorporate the butter and cheese after five minutes. Stir once more after 3 minutes of cooking.
4. Give the eggs two more minutes to finish cooking before removing them if they are done to your liking.
5. Fork it up to fluff. Serve hot.

Nutritional information
Per Serving calories: 359 protein: 19.5 g fiber: 0.0 g net carbohydrates: 1.1 g fat: 27.6 g sodium: 325 mg carbohydrates: 1.1 g sugar: 0.5 g

Cauliflower Avocado Toast

Prep Time: 15 minutes
Cook Time: 8 minutes
Serves 2

Ingredients
- 1 (12-ounce) steamer bag cauliflower
- 1 large egg
- 1/2 cup shredded mozzarella cheese
- 1 ripe medium avocado
- 1/2 teaspoon garlic powder
- 1/4 teaspoon ground black pepper

Preparation
1. Cauliflower should be prepared as directed on the package. To remove extra moisture, remove from bag and place in cheesecloth or a clean towel.
2. In a sizable bowl, combine the cauliflower with the mozzarella and egg. To fit the basket of your air fryer, cut a piece of parchment. Divide the cauliflower mixture in half, then pile it in two mounds on the parchment. Place the parchment into the air fryer basket and press the cauliflower mounds into a 1/4"-thick rectangle.
3. Set the timer for 8 minutes and raise the temperature to 400°F.
4. About halfway through the cooking process, flip the cauliflower.
5. Remove the parchment from the cauliflower and let it cool for five minutes after the timer beeps.
6. Remove the pit from the avocado, slice it open, scoop out the inside, mash it with the garlic powder and pepper, then spread it over the cauliflower.

Nutritional information
Per Serving calories: 278 protein: 14.1 g fiber: 8.2 g net carbohydrates: 7.7 g fat: 15.6 g sodium: 267 mg carbohydrates: 15.9 g sugar: 3.9 g

Air Fryer Hard-Boiled Eggs

Prep Time: 2 minutes
Cook Time: 18 minutes
Serves 4

Ingredients
- 4 large eggs
- 1 cup water

Preparation
1. Pour water over the eggs in a 4-cup round baking-safe dish. Put the dish in the basket of the air fryer.
2. Set the timer for 18 minutes and raise the temperature to 300°F.
3. When not in use, keep cooked eggs in the refrigerator or peel and eat them warm.

Nutritional information
Per Serving calories: 77 protein: 6.3 g fiber: 0.0 g net carbohydrates: 0.6 g fat: 4.4 g sodium: 62 mg carbohydrates: 0.6 g sugar: 0.6 g

Pancake Cake

Prep Time: 10 minutes
Cook Time: 7 minutes
Serves 4

Ingredients
- 1/2 cup blanched finely ground almond flour
- 1/4 cup powdered erythritol
- 1/2 teaspoon baking powder
- 2 tablespoons unsalted butter, softened
- 1 large egg
- 1/2 teaspoon unflavored gelatin
- 1/2 teaspoon vanilla extract
- 1/2 teaspoon ground cinnamon

Preparation
1. Almond flour, erythritol, and baking powder should be combined in a sizable bowl. Add butter, gelatin, cinnamon, vanilla, and egg. Add to a 6" round baking pan.
2. Put the pan in the air fryer basket.
3. The timer should be set for 7 minutes with the temperature adjusted to 300°F.
4. Cake should come out clean when tested with a toothpick to determine when it is fully cooked.

Nutritional information
Per Serving calories: 153 protein: 5.4 g fiber: 1.7 g net carbohydrates: 1.9 g sugar alcohol: 9.0 g fat: 13.4 g sodium: 80 mg carbohydrates: 12.6 g sugar: 0.6 g

Stuffed Poblanos

Prep Time: 15 minutes
Cook Time: 15 minutes
Serves 4

Ingredients
- 1/2 pound spicy ground pork breakfast sausage
- 4 large eggs
- 4 ounces full-fat cream cheese, softened
- 1/4 cup canned diced tomatoes and green chiles, drained
- 4 large poblano peppers
- 8 tablespoons shredded pepper jack cheese
- 1/2 cup full-fat sour cream

Preparation
1. Crumble and brown the ground sausage in a medium skillet over medium heat until no pink is visible. Drain the fat from the pan after removing the sausage. Scramble the eggs after cracking them into the pan until they are no longer runny.
2. Fold cream cheese into the cooked sausage after putting it in a big bowl. Tomato and chile dice should be combined. Fold the eggs in gently.
3. Cut a 4" to 5" slit in the top of each poblano and use a small knife to scrape out the seeds and white membrane. Divide the filling into four portions and carefully spoon one into each pepper. Add 2 tablespoons of pepper jack cheese to each.
4. Put a basket for the air fryer inside each pepper.
5. Set the timer for 15 minutes and raise the temperature to 350°F.
6. When ready, the cheese will be browned and the peppers will be soft. Serve immediately and top with sour cream.

Nutritional information
Per Serving calories: 489 protein: 22.8 g fiber: 3.8 g net carbohydrates: 8.8 g fat: 35.6 g sodium: 746 mg carbohydrates: 12.6 g sugar: 2.9 g

Spaghetti Squash Fritters

Prep Time: 15 minutes
Cook Time: 8 minutes
Serves 4

Ingredients
- 2 cups cooked spaghetti squash
- 2 tablespoons unsalted butter, softened
- 1 large egg
- 1/4 cup blanched finely ground almond flour
- 2 stalks green onion, sliced
- 1/2 teaspoon garlic powder
- 1 teaspoon dried parsley

Preparation
1. Using a cheesecloth or kitchen towel, drain the squash of extra moisture.
2. In a sizable bowl, combine each ingredient. Into four patties, form.
3. Cut a piece of parchment to fit the basket of your air fryer. Each patty should be placed on the parchment before going into the air fryer basket.
4. Set the timer for 8 minutes and raise the temperature to 400°F.
5. Halfway through the cooking process, flip the patties. Serve hot.

Nutritional information
Per Serving Calories: 131 protein: 3.8 g fiber: 2.0 g net carbohydrates: 5.1 g fat: 10.1 g sodium: 33 mg carbohydrates: 7.1 g sugar: 2.3 g

Sausage and Cheese Balls

Prep Time: 10 minutes
Cook Time: 12 minutes
Yields 16 balls (4 per serving)

Ingredients
- 1 pound pork breakfast sausage
- 1/2 cup shredded Cheddar cheese
- 1 ounce full-fat cream cheese, softened
- 1 large egg

Preparation
1. In a sizable bowl, combine each ingredient. 16 (1") balls should be formed. Put the balls in the basket of the air fryer.
2. Set the timer for 12 minutes and raise the temperature to 400°F.
3. During cooking, shake the basket two or three times. When fully cooked, sausage balls should be browned on the outside and have an internal temperature of at least 145°F.
4. Serve hot.

Nutritional information
Per Serving Calories: 424 protein: 22.8 g fiber: 0.0 g net carbohydrates: 1.6 g fat: 32.2 g sodium: 973 mg carbohydrates: 1.6 g sugar: 1.4 g

Cheesy Cauliflower Hash Browns

Prep Time: 20 minutes
Cook Time: 12 minutes
Serves 4

Ingredients
- 1 (12-ounce) steamer bag cauliflower
- 1 large egg
- 1 cup shredded sharp Cheddar cheese

Preparation
1. Cook the bag in the microwave in accordance with the directions on the bag. Let cauliflower cool completely before putting it in a cheesecloth or kitchen towel and wringing out the extra moisture.
2. Mash the cauliflower with a fork and mix in the cheese and egg.
3. Cut a piece of parchment to fit the basket of your air fryer. Shape a quarter of the mixture into a hash brown patty. Working in batches if necessary, place it onto the parchment and into the air fryer basket.
4. Set the timer for 12 minutes and raise the temperature to 400°F.
5. About halfway through the cooking process, flip the hash browns. They will be golden brown when fully cooked. Serve right away.

Nutritional information
Per Serving calories: 153 protein: 10.0 g fiber: 1.7 g net carbohydrates: 3.0 g fat: 9.5 g sodium: 225 mg carbohydrates: 4.7 g sugar: 1.8 g

Vegetarian Recipes

BBQ "Pulled" Mushrooms

Prep time: 5 minutes
Cook Time: 12 minutes
Serves 2

Ingredients
- 4 large portobello mushrooms
- 1 tablespoon salted butter, melted
- 1/4 teaspoon ground black pepper
- 1 teaspoon chili powder
- 1 teaspoon paprika
- 1/4 teaspoon onion powder
- 1/2 cup low-carb, sugar-free barbecue sauce

Preparation
1. Scoop out each mushroom's underside after removing the stem. Butter should be used to coat the caps before seasoning with pepper, chilli powder, paprika, and onion powder.
2. Mushrooms should be placed in the air fryer basket.
3. Set the timer for 8 minutes and raise the temperature to 400°F.
4. Remove the mushrooms from the basket when the timer beeps and set them on a cutting board or work surface. Pull the mushrooms apart with two forks, forming strands.
5. Put the mushroom strands and barbecue sauce in a 4-cup round baking dish. Put the dish in the basket of the air fryer.
6. Set the timer for 4 minutes and raise the temperature to 350°F.
7. Midway through the cooking process, stir. Serve hot.

Nutritional information
per serving calories: 108 protein: 3.3 g fiber: 2.7 g net carbohydrates: 8.2 g fat: 5.9 g sodium: 476 mg carbohydrates: 10.9 g sugar: 3.6 g

Broccoli Crust Pizza

Prep Time: 15 minutes
Cook Time: 12 minutes
Serves 4

Ingredients
- 3 cups riced broccoli, steamed and drained well
- 1 large egg
- 1/2 cup grated vegetarian Parmesan cheese
- 3 tablespoons low-carb Alfredo sauce
- 1/2 cup shredded mozzarella cheese

Preparation
1. Combine broccoli, egg, and Parmesan in a big bowl.
2. Cut a piece of parchment to fit the basket of your air fryer. Working in two batches if necessary, press out the pizza dough to fit on the parchment paper. Place in the basket of the air fryer.
3. The timer should be set for 5 minutes with the temperature adjusted to 370°F.
4. The crust should be firm enough to flip when the timer beeps. In that case, add two more minutes. Turn the crust.
5. Add mozzarella and Alfredo sauce to the top. Once more, cook in the air fryer basket for 7 more minutes, or until the cheese is golden and bubbling. Serve hot.

Nutritional information
per serving calories: 136 protein: 9.9 g fiber: 2.3 g net carbohydrates: 3.4 g fat: 7.6 g sodium: 421 mg carbohydrates: 5.7 g sugar: 1.1 g

Caprese Eggplant Stacks

Prep Time: 5 minutes
Cook Time: 12 minutes
Serves 4

Ingredients
- 1 medium eggplant, cut into 1/4" slices
- 2 large tomatoes, cut into 1/4" slices

- 4 ounces fresh mozzarella, cut into 1/2-ounce slices
- 2 tablespoons olive oil
- 1/4 cup fresh basil, sliced

Preparation
1. Four slices of eggplant should be placed on the bottom of a 6" round baking dish, followed by a slice of tomato, a slice of mozzarella, and another round of eggplant.
2. Place dish in air fryer basket, cover with foil, and drizzle with olive oil.
3. Set the timer for 12 minutes and raise the temperature to 350°F.
4. Fresh basil should be garnished with the finished dish to make the eggplant tender.

Nutritional information
Per serving calories: 195 protein: 8.5 g fiber: 5.2 g net carbohydrates: 7.5 g fat: 12.7 g sodium: 184 mg carbohydrates: 12.7 g sugar: 7.5 g

Zucchini Cauliflower Fritters

Prep Time: 15 minutes
Cook Time: 12 minutes
Serves 2

Ingredients
- 1 (12-ounce) cauliflower steamer bag
- 1 medium zucchini, shredded
- 1/4 cup almond flour
- 1 large egg
- 1/2 teaspoon garlic powder
- 1/4 cup grated vegetarian Parmesan cheese

Preparation
1. Cook the cauliflower as directed on the package, then squeeze out any extra moisture using cheesecloth or paper towels. Put into a sizable bowl.
2. Put the zucchini in the paper towel and blot the excess moisture out. Add to the cauliflower bowl. the rest of the ingredients.
3. Make four patties by evenly dividing the mixture. Place each into the air fryer basket and press into 1/4" thick patties.
4. The timer should be set for 12 minutes with the temperature adjusted to 320°F.
5. Allow fritters to cool for five minutes before moving them, then serve them warm.

Nutritional information
per serving calories: 217 protein: 13.7 g fiber: 6.5 g net carbohydrates: 8.5 g fat: 12.0 g sodium: 263 mg carbohydrates: 16.1 g sugar: 6.8 g

Air Fryer Green Beans

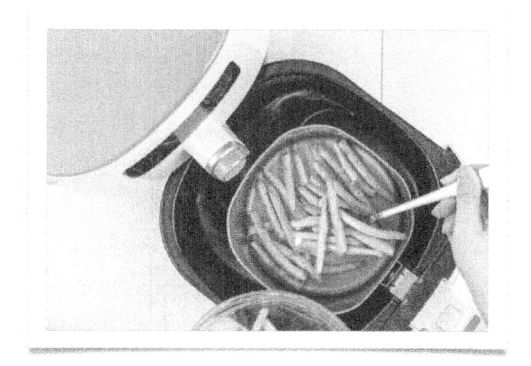

Prep Time: 5 minutes
Cook Time: 10 minutes
Total Time: 15 minutes

Ingredients
- 2 cups green beans

Preparation
1. Clean the green beans. If necessary, trim the ends.
2. Green beans are tossed in oil.
3. Green beans should be placed in an air fryer basket and cooked for 10 minutes at 390 degrees F or 198 degrees C. Enjoy!

Nutrition information
43kcal; 8g of carbohydrates; 2g of protein; 1g of fat; 1g of saturated fat; 7mg of sodium; 232mg of potassium; 3g of fibre; and 4g of sugar

Air Fryer Brussel Sprouts

Servings: 2
Prep Time: 10 minutes
Cook Time: 10 minutes
Total Time: 20 minutes

Ingredients
- 1 pound Brussels sprouts trimmed and halved
- 1 tablespoon extra virgin olive oil
- ½ teaspoon garlic powder (or minced garlic)
- 1 tablespoon balsamic vinegar
- ¼ teaspoon salt to taste

- ⅛ teaspoon freshly ground black pepper to taste

Preparation
1. Brussels sprouts should be washed in water and dried with a kitchen towel.
2. Each Brussels sprout's hard stem should be trimmed off at the bottom before cutting each sprout in half lengthwise, starting at the trimmed end.
3. Brussel sprouts should be put in a medium bowl. Garlic powder, salt, and pepper should be added along with the olive oil and balsamic vinegar. When the seasoning is evenly distributed, toss the vegetables well. The greatest method for this is to use your hands.
4. Set the air fryer's thermostat to 360°F (180°C). Spread the seasoned Brussel sprouts out in a single layer in the air fryer basket (cook in batches if required).
5. They should be crisp and faintly browned after 10 to 12 minutes of air frying at 360°F (180°C). At the midway point, shake the basket. Mine took 11 minutes to cook to perfection.
6. For a citrusy, zingy taste, drizzle some freshly squeezed lemon juice over the roasted Brussels sprouts before serving. Hot food tastes best.

Notes
Pro-Tips
- Pick Brussels sprouts that are all the same size: This facilitates efficient and uniform cooking.
- Work in groups. Ensure that the Brussels sprouts are placed in the air fryer basket in a single layer with enough room between them. If necessary, cook in batches.
- Half-shake the basket: To ensure that the broccoli florets cook evenly, jiggle the basket halfway through cooking.
- Serve them immediately: As they cool and set, these roasted Brussel sprouts go from crispy to mushy.
- Depending on the air fryer being used, the precise cooking time may change.

Variations in Seasoning
- Lemon wedges and/or zest: Just before serving, squeeze some fresh lemon juice over top.
- Cheese: After roasting, top with freshly grated Parmesan cheese.
- Herbs: Include a few handfuls of freshly chopped cilantro, parsley, or dill.
- Italian spice and red chilli flakes can be used as seasonings before roasting.

Nutritional information
Calories: 85kcal Carbohydrates: 11g Protein: 4g Fat: 4g Saturated Fat: 1g Polyunsaturated Fat: 1g Monounsaturated Fat: 3g Sodium: 175mg Potassium: 452mg Fiber: 4gSugar: 3g

Quiche-Stuffed Peppers

Prep Time: 5 minutes
Cook Time: 15 minutes
Serves 2

Ingredients
- 2 medium green bell peppers
- 3 large eggs
- 1/4 cup full-fat ricotta cheese
- 1/4 cup diced yellow onion
- 1/2 cup chopped broccoli
- 1/2 cup shredded medium Cheddar cheese

Preparation
1. Remove the peppers' tops, then use a small knife to scrape out the seeds and white membranes.
2. Combine the ricotta and eggs in a medium bowl.
3. Include broccoli and onion. Distribute the egg and vegetable mixture evenly into each pepper,. Put Cheddar on top. Fill a 4-cup round baking dish with peppers, then put the baking dish into the air fryer basket.
4. Set the timer for 15 minutes and raise the temperature to 350°F.
5. When fully cooked, eggs will be mostly firm and peppers will be tender. Serve right away.

Nutritional information
Per serving calories: 314 protein: 21.6 g fiber: 3.0 g net carbohydrates: 7.8 g fat: 18.7 g sodium: 325 mg carbohydrates: 10.8 g sugar: 4.5 g

Whole Roasted Lemon Cauliflower

Prep Time: 5 minutes
Cook Time: 15 minutes
Serves 4

Ingredients
- 1 medium head cauliflower
- 2 tablespoons salted butter, melted
- 1 medium lemon

- 1/2 teaspoon garlic powder
- 1 teaspoon dried parsley

Preparation
1. Cauliflower should have its leaves removed before being brushed with melted butter. Zest one half of the lemon onto the cauliflower after cutting it in half. Pour the zested lemon half's juice over the cauliflower after you've squeezed it.
2. Add some parsley and garlic powder. Put the head of the cauliflower in the air fryer basket.
3. Set the timer for 15 minutes and raise the temperature to 350°F.
4. Avoid overcooking cauliflower by checking it every 5 minutes. It ought to be knife-tender.
5. Pour lemon juice from the remaining half over the cauliflower before serving. Serve right away.

Nutritional information
Per Serving Calories: 91 Protein: 3.0 G Fiber: 3.2 G Net Carbohydrates: 5.2 G Fat: 5.7 G Sodium: 90 Mg Carbohydrates: 8.4 G Sugar: 3.1 G

Roasted Broccoli Salad

Prep Time: 10 minutes
Cook Time: 7 minutes
Serves 2

Ingredients
- 3 cups fresh broccoli florets
- 2 tablespoons salted butter, melted
- 1/4 cup sliced almonds
- 1/2 medium lemon

Preparation
1. Butter should be poured over the broccoli in a 6" round baking dish. Almonds should then be added, and the dish should then be placed in the air fryer basket.
2. The timer should be set for 7 minutes with the temperature adjusted to 380°F.
3. Midway through the cooking process, stir.
4. When the timer sounds, zest the lemon onto the broccoli, squeeze the juice into the pan, toss, and serve hot.

Nutritional information
Per Serving calories: 215 protein: 6.4 g fiber: 5.0 g net carbohydrates: 7.1 g fat: 16.3 g sodium: 136 mg carbohydrates: 12.1 g sugar: 3.0 g

Cheesy Zoodle Bake

Prep Time: 10 minutes
Cook Time: 8 minutes
Serves 4

Ingredients
- 2 tablespoons salted butter
- 1/4 cup diced white onion
- 1/2 teaspoon minced garlic
- 1/2 cup heavy whipping cream
- 2 ounces full-fat cream cheese
- 1 cup shredded sharp Cheddar cheese
- 2 medium zucchini, spiralized

Preparation
1. Melt butter in a sizable saucepan over medium heat. Add the onion and cook for 1-3 minutes, or until it starts to soften. After adding the garlic and cooking it for 30 seconds, adding the cream and cream cheese.
2. Stir in Cheddar after taking the pan off the heat. Put the sauce, zucchini, and other ingredients in a 4-cup round baking dish. Place the dish in the air fryer basket after covering it with foil.
3. The timer should be set for 8 minutes with the temperature adjusted to 370°F.
4. Remove the foil after 6 minutes and let the top brown for the remaining cooking time. Stir, then plate.

Nutritional information

per serving calories: 337 protein: 9.6 g fiber: 1.2 g net carbohydrates: 4.7 g fat: 28.4 g sodium: 298 mg carbohydrates: 5.9 g sugar: 4.3 g

Roasted Veggie Bowl

Prep Time: 10 minutes
Cook Time: 15 minutes
Serves 2

Ingredients
- 1 cup broccoli florets
- 1 cup quartered Brussels sprouts
- 1/2 cup cauliflower florets
- 1/4 medium white onion, peeled and sliced 1/4" thick
- 1/2 medium green bell pepper, seeded and sliced 1/4" thick
- 1 tablespoon coconut oil
- 2 teaspoons chili powder
- 1/2 teaspoon garlic powder
- 1/2 teaspoon cumin

Preparation
1. Toss all ingredients in a sizable bowl to coat the vegetables completely in oil and seasoning.
2. Vegetables should be placed in the air fryer basket.
3. Set the timer for 15 minutes and raise the temperature to 360°F.
4. While cooking, shake the pan two or three times. Serve hot.

Nutritional information
per serving calories: 121 protein: 4.3 g fiber: 5.2 g net carbohydrates: 7.9 g fat: 7.1 g sodium: 112 mg carbohydrates: 13.1 g sugar: 3.8 g

Veggie Quesadilla

Prep Time: 10 minutes
Cook Time: 5 minutes
Serves 2

Ingredients
- 1 tablespoon coconut oil
- 1/2 medium green bell pepper, seeded and chopped
- 1/4 cup diced red onion

- 1/4 cup chopped white mushrooms
- 4 flatbread dough tortillas
- 2/3 cup shredded pepper jack cheese
- 1/2 medium avocado, peeled, pitted, and mashed
- 1/4 cup full-fat sour cream
- 1/4 cup mild salsa

Preparation
1. Warm up the coconut oil in a medium skillet over medium heat. In a skillet, combine the pepper, onion, and mushrooms. Sauté for 3 to 5 minutes or until the peppers start to soften.
2. On a work surface, arrange two tortillas and top each with half a slice of cheese. Add the remaining cheese, the sautéed vegetables, and the final two tortillas to the top.
3. Carefully place the quesadillas in the air fryer basket.
4. Set the thermostat to 400°F, and then set a 5-minute timer.
5. About halfway through the cooking process, flip the quesadillas. Serve warm with salsa, avocado, and sour cream.

Nutritional information
per serving calories: 795 protein: 34.5 g fiber: 6.5 g net carbohydrates: 12.9 g fat: 61.3 g sodium: 1,051 mg carbohydrates: 19.4 g sugar: 7.4 g

Portobello Mini Pizzas

Prep Time: 10 minutes
Cook Time: 10 minutes
Serves 2

Ingredients
- 2 large portobello mushrooms
- 2 tablespoons unsalted butter, melted
- 1/2 teaspoon garlic powder
- 2/3 cup shredded mozzarella cheese
- 4 grape tomatoes, sliced
- 2 leaves fresh basil, chopped
- 1 tablespoon balsamic vinegar

Preparation
1. Simply remove the caps from the mushrooms after scooping out the interiors. Butter and garlic powder are applied to each cap.
2. Add mozzarella and tomato slices to each cap. A 6" round baking pan should be used for each mini pizza, and the pan should go into the air fryer basket.
3. The timer should be set for 10 minutes with the temperature adjusted to 380°F.
4. Pizzas should be carefully taken out of the fryer basket and topped with basil and vinegar.

Nutritional information

per serving calories: 244 protein: 10.4 g fiber: 1.4 g net carbohydrates: 5.4 g fat: 18.5 g sodium: 244 mg carbohydrates: 6.8 g sugar: 4.3 g

Three-Cheese Zucchini Boats

Prep Time: 15 minutes
Cook Time: 20 minutes
Serves 2

Ingredients
- 2 medium zucchini
- 1 tablespoon avocado oil
- 1/4 cup low-carb, no-sugar-added pasta sauce
- 1/4 cup full-fat ricotta cheese
- 1/4 cup shredded mozzarella cheese
- 1/4 teaspoon dried oregano
- 1/4 teaspoon garlic powder
- 1/2 teaspoon dried parsley
- 2 tablespoons grated vegetarian Parmesan cheese

Preparation
1. Slice each zucchini in half lengthwise, scoop out some of the inside with a spoon to make room for the filling, brush with oil, and then spoon 2 tablespoons of pasta sauce into each shell.
2. Fill each zucchini shell with the ricotta, mozzarella, oregano, garlic powder, and parsley mixture; place the filled zucchini shells in the air fryer basket.
3. Set the timer for 20 minutes and raise the temperature to 350°F.
4. Use tongs or a spatula to carefully lift the food out of the fryer basket, then sprinkle it with Parmesan before serving right away.

Nutritional information
per serving calories: 215 protein: 10.5 g fiber: 2.7 g net carbohydrates: 6.6 g fat: 14.9 g sodium: 386 mg carbohydrates: 9.3 g sugar: 5.2 g

Italian Baked Egg and Veggies

Prep Time: 10 minutes
Cook Time: 10 minutes
Serves 2

Ingredients

- 2 tablespoons salted butter
- 1 small zucchini, sliced lengthwise and quartered
- 1/2 medium green bell pepper, seeded and diced
- 1 cup fresh spinach, chopped
- 1 medium Roma tomato, diced
- 2 large eggs
- 1/4 teaspoon onion powder
- 1/4 teaspoon garlic powder
- 1/2 teaspoon dried basil
- 1/4 teaspoon dried oregano

Preparation

1. two (4") ramekins should be greased with 1 tablespoon of butter each.
2. Toss tomatoes, spinach, bell pepper, zucchini, and bell pepper in a big bowl. Place one-half of the mixture in each ramekin after dividing it in two.
3. Each ramekin should have an egg cracked on top of it, along with some oregano, basil, onion, and garlic powder. Place in the basket of the air fryer.
4. The timer should be set for 10 minutes with the temperature adjusted to 330°F.
5. Serve right away.

Nutritional information

per serving calories: 150 protein: 8.3 g fiber: 2.2 g net carbohydrates: 4.4 g fat: 10.0 g sodium: 135 mg carbohydrates: 6.6 g sugar: 3.7 g

Crustless Spinach Cheese Pie

Prep Time: 10 minutes
Cook Time: 20 minutes
Serves 4

Ingredients

- 6 large eggs
- 1/4 cup heavy whipping cream
- 1 cup frozen chopped spinach, drained
- 1 cup shredded sharp Cheddar cheese
- 1/4 cup diced yellow onion

Preparation

1. Whisk eggs in a medium bowl while adding cream to the bowl with the remaining ingredients.
2. Place into the air fryer basket in a 6" round baking dish.
3. The timer should be set for 20 minutes with the temperature adjusted to 320°F.
4. Serve eggs right away once they are cooked; they should be firm and slightly browned.

Nutritional information

per serving calories: 288 protein: 18.0 g fiber: 1.3 g net carbohydrates: 2.6 g fat: 20.0 g sodium: 322 mg carbohydrates: 3.9 g sugar: 1.5 g

Greek Stuffed Eggplant

Prep Time: 15 minutes
Cook Time: 20 minutes
Serves 2

Ingredients

- 1 large eggplant
- 2 tablespoons unsalted butter
- 1/4 medium yellow onion, diced
- 1/4 cup chopped artichoke hearts
- 1 cup fresh spinach
- 2 tablespoons diced red bell pepper
- 1/2 cup crumbled feta

Preparation

1. Slice the eggplant in half lengthwise, scoop out the flesh, and then reassemble the eggplant in its shell. Take the scooped-out eggplant, chop it, and set it aside.
2. Add butter and onion to a medium skillet set over medium heat. About 3 to 5 minutes of sautéing should soften the onions. Bell pepper, spinach, artichokes, and eggplant should all be chopped. Cook the peppers and spinach for a further five minutes, or until they soften. After taking it off the heat, gently fold in the feta.
3. Fill each eggplant shell with the filling before placing it in the air fryer basket.
4. The timer should be set for 20 minutes with the temperature adjusted to 320°F.
5. When cooked, the eggplant will be tender. Serve hot.

Nutritional information

per serving calories: 291 protein: 9.4 g fiber: 10.8 g net carbohydrates: 11.8 g fat: 18.7 g sodium: 374 mg carbohydrates: 22.6 g sugar: 12.5 g

Loaded Cauliflower Steak

Prep Time: 5 minutes
Cook Time: 7 minutes
Serves 4

Ingredients

- 1 medium head cauliflower
- 1/4 cup hot sauce
- 2 tablespoons salted butter, melted
- 1/4 cup blue cheese crumbles
- 1/4 cup full-fat ranch dressing

Preparation

1. Take the cauliflower leaves off. Slices should be about half an inch thick.
2. Brush the cauliflower with a mixture made by combining hot sauce and butter in a small bowl.
3. If necessary, fry each cauliflower steak in the air fryer in batches.
4. Set the thermostat to 400 degrees Fahrenheit and start the timer for 7 minutes.
5. The edges will start to turn dark and caramelise once they are cooked.
6. When ready to serve, top steaks with crumbled blue cheese and ranch dressing.

Nutritional information

per serving calories: 122 protein: 4.9 g fiber: 3.0 g net carbohydrates: 4.7 g fat: 8.4 g sodium: 283 mg carbohydrates: 7.7 g sugar: 2.9 g

Spicy Parmesan Artichokes

Prep Time: 10 minutes
Cook Time: 10 minutes
Serves 4

Ingredients
- 2 medium artichokes, trimmed and quartered, center removed
- 2 tablespoons coconut oil
- 1 large egg, beaten
- 1/2 cup grated vegetarian Parmesan cheese
- 1/4 cup blanched finely ground almond flour
- 1/2 teaspoon crushed red pepper flakes

Preparation
1. Artichokes should be coated in coconut oil and then dipped in beaten eggs in a big bowl.
2. In a sizable bowl, combine the Parmesan and almond flour. Add the artichoke pieces, toss to coat completely, and then top with the pepper flakes. Place in the basket of the air fryer.
3. Set the timer for 10 minutes and raise the temperature to 400°F.
4. Toss the basket around twice while cooking. Serve hot.

Nutritional information
per serving calories: 189 protein: 7.9 g fiber: 4.2 g net carbohydrates: 5.8 g fat: 13.5 g sodium: 294 mg carbohydrates: 10.0 g sugar: 0.9 g

Basic Spaghetti Squash

Prep Time: 10 minutes
Cook Time: 45 minutes
Serves 2

Ingredients
- 1/2 large spaghetti squash
- 1 tablespoon coconut oil
- 2 tablespoons salted butter, melted

- 1/2 teaspoon garlic powder
- 1 teaspoon dried parsley

Preparation
1. Apply coconut oil to the spaghetti squash's outer shell. Put the skin side down and butter the interior. Add some parsley and garlic powder.
2. Put the squash in the air fryer basket skin side down.
3. Set the timer for 30 minutes and raise the temperature to 350°F.
4. Flip the squash over so the skin side is up and cook for an additional 15 minutes, or until fork-tender, when the timer beeps. Serve hot.

Nutritional information
per serving calories: 182 protein: 1.9 g fiber: 3.9 g net carbohydrates: 14.3 g fat: 11.7 g sodium: 134 mg carbohydrates: 18.2 g sugar: 7.0 g

Cheesy Cauliflower Pizza Crust

Prep Time: 15 minutes
Cook Time: 11 minutes
Serves 2

Ingredients
- 1 (12-ounce) steamer bag cauliflower
- 1/2 cup shredded sharp Cheddar cheese
- 1 large egg
- 2 tablespoons blanched finely ground almond flour
- 1 teaspoon Italian blend seasoning

Preparation
1. Cauliflower should be prepared as directed on the package. Remove from bag and squeeze excess water out with cheesecloth or paper towels. Fill a big bowl with the cauliflower.
2. In the bowl, combine the cheese, egg, almond flour, and Italian seasoning.
3. Cut a piece of parchment to fit the basket of your air fryer. Place cauliflower in the air fryer basket after pressing it into a 6" oblong shape.
4. Set the thermostat to 360 degrees Fahrenheit and start the timer for 11 minutes.
5. Flip the pizza crust after 7 minutes.
6. Pizza should be topped as desired, put back in the air fryer basket, and cooked for a further 4 minutes, or until done and golden.

Nutritional information
per serving calories: 230 protein: 14.9 g fiber: 4.7 g net carbohydrates: 5.3 g fat: 14.2 g sodium: 257 mg carbohydrates: 10.0 g sugar: 4.2 g

FISH / SEAFOOD AIRFRYER RECIPES

Salmon Patties

Prep Time: 10 minutes
Cook Time: 8 minutes
Serves 2

Ingredients
- 2 (5-ounce) pouches cooked pink salmon
- 1 large egg
- 1/4 cup ground pork rinds
- 2 tablespoons full-fat mayonnaise
- 2 teaspoons sriracha
- 1 teaspoon chili powder

Preparation
1. Combine all the ingredients in a big bowl, then shape into four patties. Put the patties inside the air fryer basket.
2. Set the timer for 8 minutes and raise the temperature to 400°F.
3. Every patty should be carefully turned over halfway through cooking. The outside of the patties will be crisp when they are fully cooked.

Nutritional information
per serving calories: 319 protein: 33.8 g fiber: 0.5 g net carbohydrates: 1.4 g fat: 19.0 g sodium: 843 mg carbohydrates: 1.9 g sugar: 1.3 g

Spicy Salmon Jerky

Prep Time: 5 minutes
Cook Time: 4 hours
Serves 4

Ingredients
- 1 pound salmon, skin and bones removed
- 1/4 cup soy sauce (or liquid aminos)
- 1/2 teaspoon liquid smoke
- 1/4 teaspoon ground black pepper
- Juice of 1/2 medium lime
- 1/2 teaspoon ground ginger
- 1/4 teaspoon red pepper flakes

Preparation
1. Cut salmon into 4" long slices that are 1/4" thick.
2. Add the remaining ingredients to the strips that have been placed in a sizable storage bag or covered bowl. Refrigerate for two hours to allow marinating.
3. Put each strip in a single layer in the air fryer basket.
4. Set the thermostat to 140 degrees Fahrenheit, and the timer for 4 hours.
5. Let cool until you're ready to eat; store in a tight container.

Nutritional information
per serving calories: 108 protein: 15.1 g fiber: 0.2 g net carbohydrates: 0.8 g fat: 4.1 g sodium: 469 mg carbohydrates: 1.0 g sugar: 0.1 g

Air Fryer Salmon Fillets

Preparation Time: 5 minutes Cooking Time: 15 minutes
Servings: 2

Ingredients
- 1/4 cup low-fat Greek yogurt
- 2 salmon fillets
- 1 tbsp. fresh dill (chopped)
- 1 lemon juice
- 1/2 garlic powder Kosher
- salt and pepper

Preparation:
1. Place the lemon slices in the bottom of the air fryer basket.
2. Season the salmon with kosher salt and freshly ground pepper. Place the salmon on top of the lemons.
3. Allow it to cook for 15 minutes at 330°F.
4. Meanwhile, combine the garlic powder, lemon juice, salt, pepper, and dill with the yogurt.
5. Serve with the sauce.

Nutritional information:
Calories: 194 Fat: 7 g Carbs: 6 g Proteins: 25 g

Basil Parmesan Crusted Salmon

Preparation Time: 5 minutes
Cooking Time: 7 minutes
Servings: 4

Ingredients
- 3 tbsp. grated Parmesan
- 4 skinless salmon fillets
- 1/4 tsp. salt
- Freshly ground black pepper
- 3 tbsp. low-fat mayonnaise
- ¼ cup basil leaves, chopped
- 1/2 lemon
- Olive oil for spraying

Preparation
1. Preheat the air fryer to 400°F. Olive oil should be sprayed on the basket.
2. Season the salmon with salt, pepper, and lemon juice.
3. 2 tablespoons Parmesan cheese, mayonnaise, and basil leaves in a mixing dish
4. Cook for 7 minutes, or until the salmon is thoroughly cooked, with this mixture and additional Parmesan on top.
5. Serve immediately.

Nutritional information
Calories: 289 Fat: 18.5 g Carbs: 1.5 g Proteins: 30 g

Air Fryer Lobster Tails with Lemon-Garlic Butter

Prep: 10 minutes
Cook: 10 minutes
Total: 20 minutes
Servings: 2
Yield: 2 lobster tails

Ingredients
- 2 (4 ounce) lobster tails
- 4 tablespoons butter
- 1 teaspoon lemon zest
- 1 clove garlic, grated
- salt and ground black pepper to taste
- 1 teaspoon chopped fresh parsley
- 2 wedges lemon

Preparation
1. Preheat an air fryer to 380 degrees F (195 degrees C).
2. Butterfly lobster tails by cutting longitudinally through the centres of the hard top shells and flesh with kitchen shears. Cut to, but not through, the bottoms of the shells. Spread tail halves apart. Place tails in the air fryer basket with lobster flesh facing up.
3. Melt butter in a small pot over medium heat. Add lemon zest and garlic; heat until garlic is aromatic, approximately 30 seconds.
4. Transfer 2 tablespoons of butter mixture to a small dish and brush onto lobster tails; remove any remaining brushed butter to minimise contamination with raw lobster. Season lobster with salt and pepper.
5. Cook in the preheated air fryer until lobster meat is opaque, 5 to 7 minutes.
6. Spoon leftover butter from the skillet over lobster meat. Top with parsley and serve with lemon wedges.

Nutritional information
Per Serving: 313 calories; protein 18.1g; carbs 3.3g; fat 25.8g; cholesterol 128.7mg; sodium 590.4mg.

Air Fryer Shrimp and Polenta

Prep: 15 minutes
Cook: 30 minutes
Total: 45 minutes
Serving: 2
Yield: 2 servings

Ingredients

- ½ (16 ounce) tube polenta, sliced into 6 rounds
- 2 teaspoons extra-virgin olive oil, divided
- salt and ground black pepper to taste
- 8 ounces thawed frozen jumbo shrimp—drained, peeled, and deveined
- 12 grape tomatoes
- 2 tablespoons unsalted butter, softened
- 2 teaspoons chopped fresh parsley
- 1 teaspoon hot pepper sauce
- ½ teaspoon lemon-pepper seasoning

Preparation

1. Achieve a 400°F air fryer temperature.
2. Arrange polenta rounds on a spotless work surface. Apply 1 teaspoon of olive oil on each side, sprinkle with salt, and set away.
3. Mix tomatoes and shrimp in a bowl. Stir in the final 1 teaspoon of olive oil. Use tongs to add tomatoes to the air fryer's basket.
4. Cook tomatoes for about two minutes in the preheated air fryer or until they are blistered. Crush tomatoes with a wooden spoon after transferring them to a big bowl.
5. Put shrimp in the air fryer's basket and fry for 10 minutes. Adding the shrimp to the tomato-crushed dish is a good idea.
6. Rounds of polenta should be placed in the air fryer basket and cooked for 15 minutes. Cook for another 15 minutes on the flip side, or until golden brown.
7. Butter, parsley, hot pepper sauce, and lemon-pepper spice are combined in a bowl while the polenta rounds are cooking.
8. Place the polenta cakes on two serving dishes. Serve with seasoned butter and tomato-shrimp mixture spooned on top.

Nutritional information

Per Serving: 331 calories; protein 21.5g; carbs 21.8g; fat 17.5g; cholesterol 200.2mg; sodium 808.1mg.

Air Fryer Lemon Pepper Shrimp

Prep: 5 minutes
Cook: 10 minutes
Total: 15 minutes
Servings: 2

Ingredient
- 1 tablespoon olive oil
- 1 lemon, juiced
- 1 teaspoon lemon pepper
- ¼ teaspoon paprika
- ¼ teaspoon garlic powder
- 12 ounces uncooked medium shrimp, peeled and deveined
- 1 lemon, sliced

Preparation
1. As directed by the manufacturer, heat the air fryer to 400 degrees F.
2. Mix the oil, paprika, garlic powder, lemon juice, and lemon pepper in a bowl. Add the shrimp and coat well.
3. Cook shrimp in the preheated air fryer for 6 to 8 minutes, or until the flesh is opaque and the shrimp are brilliant pink on the outside. Add lemon wedges to the dish.

Nutritional information
Per Serving: 215 calories; protein 28.9g; carbohydrates 12.6g; fat 8.6g; cholesterol 255.4mg; sodium 528 mg

Cilantro Lime Baked Salmon

Prep Time: 10 minutes
Cook Time: 12 minutes
Serves 2

Ingredients
- 2 (3-ounce) salmon fillets, skin removed
- 1 tablespoon salted butter, melted
- 1 teaspoon chili powder
- 1/2 teaspoon finely minced garlic
- 1/4 cup sliced pickled jalapeños
- 1/2 medium lime, juiced
- 2 tablespoons chopped cilantro

Preparation
1. Salmon fillets should be placed in a 6" round baking pan, brushed with butter, and sprinkled with garlic and chilli powder.
2. Pour half of the lime juice over the salmon, cover with foil, and place pan into air fryer basket. Place jalapeno slices on top and all around salmon.
3. The timer should be set for 12 minutes with the temperature adjusted to 370°F.
4. Salmon should be easily flaked with a fork and have an internal temperature of at least 145°F when fully cooked.
5. Serve with cilantro as a garnish and spritz with the remaining lime juice.

Nutritional information
per serving calories: 167 protein: 15.8 g fiber: 0.7 g net carbohydrates: 0.9 g fat: 9.9 g sodium: 248 mg carbohydrates: 1.6 g sugar: 0.2 g

Buttery Cod

Prep Time: 5 minutes
Cook Time: 8 minutes
Serves 2

Ingredients
- 2 (4-ounce) cod fillets
- 2 tablespoons salted butter, melted
- 1 teaspoon Old Bay seasoning
- 1/2 medium lemon, sliced

Preparation
1. Cod fillets should be placed in a 6" round baking dish. Each fillet should be brushed with butter, sprinkled with Old Bay seasoning, and given two slices of lemon. The baking dish should then be covered in foil and placed in the air fryer basket.
2. Set the timer for 8 minutes and raise the temperature to 350°F.
3. When finished, the internal temperature should be at least 145°F, and it should be served warm.

Nutritional information
per serving calories: 179 protein: 17.4 g fiber: 0.0 g net carbohydrates: 0.0 g fat: 11.1 g sodium: 714 mg carbohydrates: 0.0 g sugar: 0.0 g

Shrimp Kebabs

Prep Time: 10 minutes
Cook Time: 7 minutes
Serves 2

Ingredients
- 18 medium shelled and deveined shrimp
- 1 medium zucchini, cut into 1" cubes
- 1/2 medium red bell pepper, cut into 1"-thick squares
- 1/4 medium red onion, cut into 1"-thick squares
- 11/2 tablespoons coconut oil, melted
- 2 teaspoons chili powder
- 1/2 teaspoon paprika
- 1/4 teaspoon ground black pepper

Preparation
1. Four bamboo skewers (6") should be soaked in water for 30 minutes. arrange a shrimp, zucchini, pepper, and onion on the skewer. Continue until all ingredients have been used.
2. Oiled with coconut, each kebab is brushed. Add some black pepper, paprika, and chilli powder. Kebabs should be placed in the air fryer basket.
3. Set the temperature to 400 degrees Fahrenheit, and cook the shrimp and vegetables for 7 minutes, or until they are done.
4. Midway through the cooking process, flip the kebabs. Serve hot.

Nutritional information
per serving calories: 166 protein: 9.5 g fiber: 3.1 g net carbohydrates: 5.4 g fat: 10.7 g sodium: 391 mg carbohydrates: 8.5 g sugar: 4.5 g

Sesame-Crusted Tuna Steak

Prep Time: 5 minutes
Cook Time: 8 minutes
Serves 2

Ingredients
- 2 (6-ounce) tuna steaks
- 1 tablespoon coconut oil, melted
- 1/2 teaspoon garlic powder
- 2 teaspoons white sesame seeds
- 2 teaspoons black sesame seeds

Preparation
1. Coconut oil should be used to brush each tuna steak before adding garlic powder.
2. Sesame seeds should be combined in a big bowl before being used to coat each tuna steak as completely as possible. Tuna steaks should be placed in the air fryer basket.
3. Set the timer for 8 minutes and raise the temperature to 400°F.
4. About halfway through the cooking process, flip the steaks. At an internal temperature of 145°F, steaks are well-done. Serve hot.

Nutritional information
per serving calories: 280 protein: 42.7 g fiber: 0.8 g net carbohydrates: 1.2 g fat: 10.0 g sodium: 77 mg carbohydrates: 2.0 g sugar: 0.0 g

Crab Cakes

Prep Time: 10 minutes
Cook Time: 10 minutes
Serves 4

Ingredients
- 2 (6-ounce) cans lump crabmeat
- 1/4 cup blanched finely ground almond flour
- 1 large egg
- 2 tablespoons full-fat mayonnaise
- 1/2 teaspoon Dijon mustard
- 1/2 tablespoon lemon juice

- 1/2 medium green bell pepper, seeded and chopped
- 1/4 cup chopped green onion
- 1/2 teaspoon Old Bay seasoning

Preparation
1. All ingredients should be combined in a big bowl. Create four balls, then patties by spreading them out. Put the air fryer basket with the patties inside.
2. Set the timer for 10 minutes and raise the temperature to 350°F.
3. Flip the patties halfway through cooking. Serve hot.

Nutritional information

per serving calories: 151 protein: 13.4 g fiber: 0.9 g net carbohydrates: 1.4 g fat: 10.0 g sodium: 467 mg carbohydrates: 2.3 g sugar: 0.5 g

Fish Taco Bowl With Jalapeño Slaw

Prep Time: 10 minutes
Cook Time: 10 minutes
Serves 2

Ingredients
- 1 cup shredded cabbage
- 1/4 cup full-fat sour cream
- 2 tablespoons full-fat mayonnaise
- 1/4 cup chopped pickled jalapeños
- 2 (3-ounce) cod fillets
- 1 teaspoon chili powder
- 1 teaspoon cumin
- 1/2 teaspoon paprika
- 1/4 teaspoon garlic powder
- 1 medium avocado, peeled, pitted, and sliced
- 1/2 medium lime

Preparation
1. Place the cabbage, sour cream, mayonnaise, and jalapenos in a sizable bowl. Mix thoroughly until coated. Place in the refrigerator and let sit for 20 minutes.
2. Chili powder, cumin, paprika, and garlic powder should be added to the cod fillets. Put a basket for the air fryer on each fillet.
3. The timer should be set for 10 minutes with the temperature adjusted to 370°F.
4. Halfway through the cooking process, flip the fillets. Fish should be fully cooked when the internal temperature reaches at least 145°F.
5. To serve, divide the slaw mixture between two bowls, top with avocado and cod fillets that have been broken into pieces. In each bowl, squirt lime juice on top. Serve right away.

Nutritional information

per serving calories: 342 protein: 16.1 g fiber: 6.4 g net carbohydrates: 5.3 g fat: 25.2 g sodium: 587 mg carbohydrates: 11.7 g sugar: 2.8 g

Fried Tuna Salad Bites

Prep Time: 10 minutes
Cook Time: 7 minutes
Yields 12 bites (3 per serving)

Ingredients
- 1 (10-ounce) can tuna, drained
- 1/4 cup full-fat mayonnaise
- 1 stalk celery, chopped
- 1 medium avocado, peeled, pitted, and mashed
- 1/2 cup blanched finely ground almond flour, divided
- 2 teaspoons coconut oil

Preparation
1. Combine tuna, mayonnaise, celery, and mashed avocado in a big bowl. Create balls out of the mixture.
2. Coconut oil spray is applied after rolling balls in almond flour. Put the air fryer basket with the balls inside.
3. Set the thermostat to 400 degrees Fahrenheit and start the timer for 7 minutes.
4. After five minutes, gently turn the tuna bites. Serve hot.

Nutritional information
per serving calories: 323 protein: 17.3 g fiber: 4.0 g net carbohydrates: 2.3 g fat: 25.4 g sodium: 311 mg carbohydrates: 6.3 g sugar: 0.8 g

Tuna Zoodle Casserole

Prep Time: 15 minutes
Cook Time: 15 minutes
Serves 4

Ingredients
- 2 tablespoons salted butter
- 1/4 cup diced white onion
- 1/4 cup chopped white mushrooms
- 2 stalks celery, finely chopped
- 1/2 cup heavy cream
- 1/2 cup vegetable broth
- 2 tablespoons full-fat mayonnaise
- 1/4 teaspoon xanthan gum
- 1/2 teaspoon red pepper flakes

- 2 medium zucchini, spiralized
- 2 (5-ounce) cans albacore tuna
- 1 ounce pork rinds, finely ground

Preparation
1. Melt butter in a sizable saucepan over medium heat. Add the celery, onion, and mushrooms and sauté for 3 to 5 minutes, or until fragrant.
2. Add the mayonnaise, heavy cream, vegetable broth, and xanthan gum. Reduce the heat and cook the mixture for an additional three minutes or until it starts to thicken.
3. Include tuna, zucchini, and red pepper flakes. After stirring the zucchini noodles until coated, turn off the heat.
4. Pour into a round 4-cup baking dish. Place a layer of ground pork rinds on top and cover with foil. Place in the basket of the air fryer.
5. The timer should be set for 15 minutes with the temperature adjusted to 370°F.
6. Remove the foil after 3 minutes has passed so that the casserole's top can brown. Serve hot.

Nutritional information
per serving calories: 339 protein: 19.7 g fiber: 1.8 g net carbohydrates: 4.3 g fat: 25.1 g sodium: 522 mg carbohydrates: 6.1 g sugar: 4.1 g

Crab Legs

Prep Time: 5 minutes
Cook Time: 15 minutes
Serves 4

Ingredients
- 1/4 cup salted butter, melted and divided
- 3 pounds crab legs
- 1/4 teaspoon garlic powder
- Juice of 1/2 medium lemon

Preparation
1. Pour 2 tablespoons of butter over the crab legs in a big bowl. Crab legs should be placed in the air fryer basket.
2. Set the timer for 15 minutes and raise the temperature to 400°F.
3. Halfway through the cooking process, shake the air fryer basket and toss the crab legs.
4. Combine the remaining butter, garlic powder, and lemon juice in a small bowl.
5. Remove the meat from the crab legs before serving. With lemon butter, dip.

Nutritional information
per serving calories: 123 protein: 15.7 g fiber: 0.0 g net carbohydrates: 0.4 g fat: 5.6 g sodium: 756 mg carbohydrates: 0.4 g sugar: 0.1 g

Foil-Packet Salmon

Prep Time: 10 minutes
Cook Time: 12 minutes
Serves 2

Ingredients
- 2 (4-ounce) salmon fillets, skin removed
- 2 tablespoons unsalted butter, melted
- 1/2 teaspoon garlic powder
- 1 medium lemon
- 1/2 teaspoon dried dill

Preparation
1. Put each fillet on a square of aluminium foil measuring 5" by 5". Sprinkle with garlic powder and drizzle with butter.
2. Lemon zest the other half, then sprinkle it over the salmon. Lay two slices of the remaining lemon half on each piece of salmon. Dill should be added to salmon.
3. To completely close packets, gather and fold the foil at the top and sides. Foil packets should be placed in the air fryer basket.
4. When fully cooked, salmon will be easily flaked and have an internal temperature of at least 145°F. Serve right away.

Nutritional information
per serving calories: 252 protein: 20.9 g fiber: 0.4 g net carbohydrates: 0.8 g fat: 16.5 g sodium: 47 mg carbohydrates: 1.2 g sugar: 0.2 g

Coconut Shrimp

Prep Time: 5 minutes
Cook Time: 6 minutes
Serves 2

Ingredients
- 8 ounces medium shelled and deveined shrimp
- 2 tablespoons salted butter, melted
- 1/2 teaspoon Old Bay seasoning
- 1/4 cup unsweetened shredded coconut

Preparation
1. The shrimp should be mixed with butter and Old Bay seasoning in a big bowl.
2. Put coconut shreds in a bowl. Place the shrimp in the air fryer basket after covering each piece with coconut.
3. Set the timer for 6 minutes and raise the temperature to 400°F.
4. Halfway through the cooking period, turn the shrimp gently. Serve right away.

Nutritional information
per serving calories: 252 protein: 16.9 g fiber: 2.0 g net carbohydrates: 1.8 g fat: 17.8 g sodium: 902 mg carbohydrates: 3.8 g sugar: 0.7 g

Lemon Garlic Shrimp

Prep Time: 5 minutes
Cook Time: 6 minutes
Serves 2

Ingredients
- 1 medium lemon
- 8 ounces medium shelled and deveined shrimp
- 2 tablespoons unsalted butter, melted
- 1/2 teaspoon Old Bay seasoning
- 1/2 teaspoon minced garlic

Preparation
1. lemon, then cut in half after zesting. In a large bowl, add the shrimp and top with the juice of 1/2 a lemon.
2. Add the remaining ingredients to the bowl along with the lemon zest. Once completely coated, toss the shrimp.
3. Fill a 6" round baking dish with the contents of the bowl, then put it in the air fryer basket.
4. Set the timer for 6 minutes and raise the temperature to 400°F.
5. When fully cooked, shrimp will be a bright pink colour; serve warm with pan sauce.

Nutritional information
per serving calories: 190 protein: 16.4 g fiber: 0.4 g net carbohydrates: 2.5 g fat: 11.8 g sodium: 812 mg carbohydrates: 2.9 g sugar: 0.5 g

Almond Pesto Salmon

Prep Time: 5 minutes
Cook Time: 12 minutes
Serves 2

Ingredients
- 1/4 cup pesto
- 1/4 cup sliced almonds, roughly chopped
- 2 (11/2"-thick) salmon fillets (about 4 ounces each)
- 2 tablespoons unsalted butter, melted

Preparation
1. Combine almonds and pesto in a small bowl. Place aside.
2. Fillets should be placed in a 6" round baking dish.
3. Place the dish into the air fryer basket, brushing each fillet with butter and topping each with half of the pesto mixture.
4. Set the timer for 12 minutes and raise the temperature to 390°F.
5. When fully cooked and has attained an internal temperature of at least 145°F, salmon will flake easily.

Nutritional information
per serving calories: 433 protein: 23.3 g fiber: 2.4 g net carbohydrates: 3.7 g fat: 34.0 g sodium: 341 mg carbohydrates: 6.1 g sugar: 0.9 g

Crispy Fish Sticks

Prep Time: 15 minutes
Cook Time: 10 minutes
Serves 4 (4 sticks per serving)

Ingredients
- 1 ounce pork rinds, finely ground
- 1/4 cup blanched finely ground almond flour
- 1/2 teaspoon Old Bay seasoning
- 1 tablespoon coconut oil
- 1 large egg
- 1 pound cod fillet, cut into 3/4" strips

Preparation

1. Mix together in a sizable bowl the ground pork rinds, almond flour, Old Bay seasoning, and coconut oil. Whisk the egg in a medium bowl.
2. Each fish stick should be dipped into the egg, gently pressed into the flour mixture, and coated as completely and uniformly as possible. Put the air fryer basket with the fish sticks inside.
3. Set the timer for 10 minutes or until golden, and adjust the heat to 400°F.
4. Serve right away.

Nutritional information

per serving calories: 205 protein: 24.4 g fiber: 0.8 g net carbohydrates: 0.8 g fat: 10.7 g sodium: 547 mg carbohydrates: 1.6 g sugar: 0.3 g

Poultry Recipes

Spinach and Feta-Stuffed Chicken Breast

Prep Time: 15 minutes
Cook Time: 25 minutes
Serves 2

Ingredients

- 1 tablespoon unsalted butter
- 5 ounces frozen spinach, thawed and drained
- 1/2 teaspoon garlic powder, divided
- 1/2 teaspoon salt, divided
- 1/4 cup chopped yellow onion
- 1/4 cup crumbled feta
- 2 (6-ounce) boneless, skinless chicken breasts
- 1 tablespoon coconut oil

Preparation

1. Sauté spinach for three minutes in butter in a medium skillet over medium heat. Add onion to the pan, then sprinkle spinach with 1/4 teaspoon each of salt and garlic powder.
2. 3 more minutes of sautéing is followed by removal from heat and placement in a medium bowl. Combine feta with the spinach mixture.
3. Place the chicken breasts into the air fryer basket, season with the remaining salt and garlic powder, and cut a 4" slit lengthwise into the side of each chicken breast. Spoon half of the mixture into each piece and fasten with a few toothpicks.
4. Set the timer for 25 minutes and raise the temperature to 350°F.
5. Chicken should be golden brown and at least 165°F internally when fully cooked. Slice and serve while still warm.

Nutritional information

per serving calories: 393 protein: 43.9 g fiber: 2.5 g net carbohydrates: 3.7 g fat: 18.5 g sodium: 882 mg carbohydrates: 6.2 g sugar: 2.1 g

Air Fryer Low Carb Nashville Hot Chicken Sandwich

Prep Time 10 minutes
Cook Time 12 minutes
Resting Time 1 hour
Total Time 1 hour 22 minutes
Serving 4 People

Ingredients
Spice Blend
- 3-5 tablespoon cayenne pepper see notes about spiciness
- 1 teaspoon paprika
- 1 teaspoon chili powder
- 2 tablespoon swerve brown sugar erythritol
- 1 teaspoon garlic powder
- ⅛ teaspoon salt
- ⅛ teaspoon black pepper

Chicken Thighs
- 4 skinless boneless chicken thighs
- 1 large egg
- ½ cup butter milk
- 1 tablespoon franks red hot sauce
- ½ cup pork rind crumbs
- ½ cup almond flour
- ⅛ teaspoon salt
- ⅛ teaspoon black pepper
- 4 tablespoon melted butter for adding to half of the spice blend to coat the cooked chicken thighs

Preparation
1. Spice mixture
2. In a small bowl, combine the seasonings and swerve brown sugar.
3. The other half of the spice mixture should be applied on both sides of the chicken thighs. Keep chilled for one hour in a closed container.
4. After an hour, remove the chicken from the refrigerator.
5. Set the air fryer to 400°F before using it (see notes for oven method).
6. Mix the one egg, buttermilk, and spicy sauce in a single shallow basin. Combine the almond flour, pork rind crumbs, salt, and pepper in a separate shallow basin.
7. Each chicken thigh should be well covered after being dipped in the egg mixture. After that, dredge it in the breadcrumb mixture so that both sides are well coated.
8. Each chicken thigh should be placed in the air fryer basket after being sprayed with cooking spray. Apply cooking spray sparingly to the tops of the chicken thighs. After using the air fryer for 8 minutes on each side, reapply the cooking spray to each side and continue air frying for 2 more minutes.
9. Place on a clean wire rack that is set on a baking sheet after gently removing from the air

fryer. Mix the remaining spice mix with the melted butter and spread the paste over the chicken thighs. Add extra melted butter if the paste is too thick.

10. You may serve chicken thighs on their own or with pickles, lettuce, and mayo on a low-carb hamburger bun.

Nutritional information

Amount per Serving: 1 Thigh per serving
496 Calories 28g Carbohydrates, 31g Fat 2g Sugar, 6g Fiber, and 2g Protein 52 g

Cilantro Lime Chicken Thighs

Prep Time: 15 minutes
Cook Time: 22 minutes
Serves 4

Ingredients

- 4 bone-in, skin-on chicken thighs
- 1 teaspoon baking powder
- 1/2 teaspoon garlic powder
- 2 teaspoons chili powder
- 1 teaspoon cumin
- 2 medium limes
- 1/4 cup chopped fresh cilantro

Preparation

1. Sprinkle baking powder over chicken thighs after patting them dry.
2. Garlic powder, chilli powder, and cumin should be combined in a small bowl before being sprinkled evenly over chicken thighs and gently rubbed in.
3. Slice a lime in half, then rub the juice over the thighs. Chicken should be placed in the air fryer basket.
4. The timer should be set for 22 minutes with the temperature adjusted to 380°F.
5. For serving, slice the remaining lime into four wedges and top the cooked chicken with the garnish of cilantro.

Nutritional information

per serving calories: 435 protein: 32.3 g fiber: 0.6 g net carbohydrates: 2.0 g fat: 29.1 g sodium: 317 mg carbohydrates: 2.6 g sugar: 0.3 g

Air Fryer Buttermilk Fried Chicken

Prep time: 25 minutes
Servings 4
Serving size 1 (4 oz) piece of chicken

Ingredients
- low-fat buttermilk 1/3 cup
- hot sauce 1/4 tsp
- boneless, skinless chicken breasts (cut in half lengthwise to make 4 equal portions) 1 lb
- corn flakes 6 tbsp
- stone-ground cornmeal 3 tbsp
- garlic powder 1 tsp
- paprika 1 tsp
- Salt 1/4 tsp
- coarse-ground black pepper 1/4 tsp
- nonstick cooking spray 1

Preparation
1. Mix the spicy sauce and buttermilk in a small, deep basin. The chicken should be placed in the buttermilk mixture. Let it stand for 15 minutes.
2. Advertisement
3. Put the cornflakes in the food processor's work bowl. Process until pebble-like crumbs appear. Pulse to combine the cornmeal, paprika, salt, and pepper after adding the remaining ingredients. Crumbs should be poured into a small basin. (If you don't have a food processor, you may use a rolling pin to crush the cornflakes in a plastic bag.)
4. Allow the extra buttermilk to trickle back into the basin while you drain the chicken. Sprinkle the cornflakes equally over the chicken pieces. Put the chicken pieces on a wire rack after coating.
5. Chicken should be put in the air fryer basket. Spray with nonstick cooking spray for 2 seconds (if all the chicken won't fit, fry it in batches to avoid crowding). The air fryer should be on for 7 minutes at 375°F. Turn the chunks of chicken. Until the chicken is cooked through and a meat thermometer placed in the middle reads 165°F, continue to air fry for an additional 7 to 10 minutes.

Nutritional information Amount per serving
160 calories, 3.5 grams of total fat, 0.8 grams of saturated fat, and 0 grams of trans fat, 7 grams of dietary fibre, and 24 grams of protein.

Crispy Buffalo Chicken Tenders

Prep Time: 15 minutes
Cook Time: 20 minutes
Serves 4

Ingredients
- 1 pound boneless, skinless chicken tenders
- 1/4 cup hot sauce
- 1 1/2 ounces pork rinds, finely ground
- 1 teaspoon chili powder
- 1 teaspoon garlic powder

Preparation
1. Put chicken tenders in a big bowl and cover them with hot sauce. Sprinkle hot sauce evenly over the tenders.
2. Grinded pork rinds should be combined with garlic and chilli powder in a separate, big bowl.
3. Each tender should be fully covered in the ground pork rinds. Press the pork rinds into the chicken by wetting your hands with water.
4. Put the tenders in the air fryer basket in a single layer.
5. Set the timer for 20 minutes and raise the temperature to 375°F.
6. Serve hot.

Nutritional information
per serving calories: 160 protein: 27.3 g fiber: 0.4 g net carbohydrates: 0.6 g fat: 4.4 g sodium: 387 mg carbohydrates: 1.0 g sugar: 0.1 g

Italian Chicken Thighs

Prep Time: 5 minutes
Cook Time: 20 minutes
Serves 2

Ingredients

- 4 bone-in, skin-on chicken thighs
- 2 tablespoons unsalted butter, melted
- 1 teaspoon dried parsley
- 1 teaspoon dried basil
- 1/2 teaspoon garlic powder
- 1/4 teaspoon onion powder
- 1/4 teaspoon dried oregano

Preparation

1. The remaining ingredients should be sprinkled over the butter-brushed chicken thighs. Thighs should be put into the air fryer basket.
2. The timer should be set for 20 minutes with the temperature adjusted to 380°F.
3. Flip the thighs over halfway through the cooking process.
4. When fully cooked, the interior should be at least 165°F, and the skin should be crisp. Serve hot.

Nutritional information

per serving calories: 596 protein: 68.3 g fiber: 0.4 g net carbohydrates: 0.8 g fat: 30.9 g sodium: 292 mg carbohydrates: 1.2 g sugar: 0.1 g

Air Fryer Buffalo Chicken Meatballs

Prep Time: 10 minutes
Cook Time: 20 minutes
Total Time: 30 minutes
Yield: 4

INGREDIENTS

- 1 pound of ground chicken
- 1/2 cup plain bread crumbs
- 1 egg
- 1/4 cup finely chopped celery
- 1 tsp minced garlic
- 1/2 tsp salt
- 1 cup buffalo sauce
- 1/4 cup ranch dressing
- 2 Tbsp. unsalted butter
- blue cheese crumbles
- chopped chives for garnish
- appetizer toothpicks

Preparation

1. Unsalted butter, ranch dressing, and buffalo sauce are combined in a skillet and heated over medium-low heat while being intermittently stirred. Once everything is well blended, turn heat down to low and keep heated until needed.
2. Add the ground chicken, bread crumbs, egg, chopped celery, garlic powder, and salt to a mixing bowl. Mix everything together thoroughly with your hands.
3. Make 1-inch balls of the chicken mixture, roll them in frying spray or oil, and then set them in the air fryer basket. Make sure to give them some space.
4. 20 minutes of air frying at 400 degrees Fahrenheit. Place the meatballs on a platter after removing them from the air fryer basket.
5. I've listed my favourite toothpick appetizer below. After dipping each meatball in the buffalo sauce, set it on your serving tray. Do this procedure once more for each meatball.
6. Serve right away after adding blue cheese crumbles and chives.

Almond-Crusted Chicken

Prep Time: 15 minutes
Cook Time: 25 minutes
Serves 4

Ingredients
- 1/4 cup slivered almonds
- 2 (6-ounce) boneless, skinless chicken breasts
- 2 tablespoons full-fat mayonnaise
- 1 tablespoon Dijon mustard

Preparation
1. The almonds should be finely chopped or processed in a food processor. Almonds should be distributed evenly on a plate.
2. Each chicken breast should be cut in half lengthwise.
3. Chicken should be coated with a mixture made by combining the mayonnaise and mustard in a small bowl.
4. To completely cover, place each piece of chicken in the chopped almonds. Put the pieces into the air fryer basket with care.
5. Set the timer for 25 minutes and raise the temperature to 350°F.
6. When the internal temperature of the chicken reaches 165°F or higher, it is considered to be done. Serve hot.

Nutritional information
per serving calories: 195 protein: 20.9 g fiber: 0.8 g net carbohydrates: 1.0 g fat: 10.1 g sodium: 175 mg carbohydrates: 1.8 g sugar: 0.3 g

Honey Balsamic Air Fryer Chicken Thighs

Prep Time: 10 minutes
Cook Time: 20 minutes
Marinating Time: 1 hour
Total Time: 1 hour 30 minutes
Servings: 4

Ingredients

- ⅓ cup fresh orange juice
- 1 tablespoon + 2 teaspoons balsamic vinegar
- 1 tablespoon + 2 teaspoons honey
- ¾ teaspoon Dijon mustard
- ½ teaspoon kosher salt
- ¼ teaspoon ground pepper
- 8 (about 28 oz.) boneless, skinless chicken thighs trimmed
- 1 tablespoon minced flat-leaf parsley

Preparation

1. Combine the orange juice, balsamic vinegar, honey, Dijon mustard, salt, and pepper in a glass or ceramic bowl. 1/4 cup of the sauce should be saved.
2. The leftover marinade should be added to the bowl containing the chicken. Chicken is coated by tossing. Chicken should be covered, marinated, and refrigerated for at least an hour and maybe overnight.
3. Preheat air fryer to 400 degrees Fahrenheit.
4. Place half of the chicken in the air fryer basket in a single layer. Cook for about 10 minutes total, rotating the chicken halfway through, until the chicken is well done. Use the leftover chicken in the same manner.
5. Pour the 1/4 cup saved marinade into a small saucepan over medium heat while the chicken cooks. Cook for 3 to 4 minutes, stirring often, until the glaze starts to slightly decrease.
6. Sprinkle the parsley on top after drizzling the glaze over the chicken. Serve.

Nutritional information

Serving: 2 thighs, calories 276.4kcal, 10.2g carbs, 39.2g protein, 7.8g fat, 2g saturated fat, 164.5mg cholesterol, 336.2mg sodium, 0.1g fibre, and 8.9g sugar

Chicken Pizza Crust

Prep Time: 10 minutes
Cook Time: 25 minutes
Serves 4

Ingredients
- 1 pound ground chicken thigh meat
- 1/4 cup grated Parmesan cheese
- 1/2 cup shredded mozzarella

Preparation
1. Combine all ingredients in a sizable bowl. Divide into four equal pieces.
2. Each portion of the chicken mixture should be spread out onto one of the four parchment circles that measure 6" in diameter. Working in batches as necessary, place into the air fryer basket.
3. Set the timer for 25 minutes and raise the temperature to 375°F.
4. Halfway through the cooking process, flip the crust.
5. When it is fully cooked, you can add cheese and your preferred toppings, and cook for an additional five minutes. Or you can freeze or refrigerate the crust and top it when you're ready to eat.

Nutritional information
per serving calories: 230 protein: 24.7 g fiber: 0.0 g net carbohydrates: 1.2 g fat: 12.8 g sodium: 268 mg carbohydrates: 1.2 g sugar: 0.2 g

Blackened Cajun Chicken Tenders

Prep Time: 10 minutes
Cook Time: 17 minutes
Serves 4

Ingredients
- 2 teaspoons paprika
- 1 teaspoon chili powder
- 1/2 teaspoon garlic powder
- 1/2 teaspoon dried thyme
- 1/4 teaspoon onion powder
- 1/8 teaspoon ground cayenne pepper
- 2 tablespoons coconut oil

- 1 pound boneless, skinless chicken tenders
- 1/4 cup full-fat ranch dressing

Preparation
1. Combine all the seasonings in a small bowl.
2. After liberally coating each tender in the spice mixture, drizzle oil over the chicken tenders. Put the air fryer basket with the tenders inside.
3. The timer should be set for 17 minutes with the temperature adjusted to 375°F.
4. 165°F will be the internal temperature of fully cooked tenders. Ranch dressing should be available for dipping.

Nutritional information

per serving calories: 163 protein: 21.2 g fiber: 0.8 g net carbohydrates: 0.7 g fat: 7.5 g sodium: 132 mg carbohydrates: 1.5 g sugar: 0.2 g

Lemon Pepper Drumsticks

Prep Time: 5 minutes
Cook Time: 25 minutes
Yields 8 drumsticks (2 per serving)

Ingredients
- 2 teaspoons baking powder
- 1/2 teaspoon garlic powder
- 8 chicken drumsticks
- 4 tablespoons salted butter, melted
- 1 tablespoon lemon pepper seasoning

Preparation
1. Garlic and baking powder should be applied to the chicken skin and sprinkled over the drumsticks. Drumsticks should be placed in the air fryer basket.
2. Set the timer for 25 minutes and raise the temperature to 375°F.
3. Use tongs to turn the drumsticks halfway through cooking.
4. Remove from fryer when skin is golden and internal temperature reaches at least 165°F.
5. Mix the butter and lemon pepper seasoning in a big bowl. Drumsticks should be added to the bowl and coated. Serve hot.

Nutritional information

per serving calories: 532 protein: 48.3 g fiber: 0.0 g net carbohydrates: 1.2 g fat: 32.3 g sodium: 706 mg carbohydrates: 1.2 g sugar: 0.0 g

Jalapeño Popper Hasselback Chicken

Prep Time: 20 minutes
Cook Time: 20 minutes
Serves 2

Ingredients

- 4 slices sugar-free bacon, cooked and crumbled
- 2 ounces full-fat cream cheese, softened
- 1/2 cup shredded sharp Cheddar cheese, divided
- 1/4 cup sliced pickled jalapeños
- 2 (6-ounce) boneless, skinless chicken breasts

Preparation

1. Place the cooked bacon in a medium bowl, then stir in the cream cheese, the first half of the Cheddar, and the jalapeno slices.
2. Making sure not to cut all the way through, make slits in each of the chicken breasts about 3/4 of the way across the chicken. You'll probably have 6–8 slits per chicken breast, depending on its size.
3. Insert the cream cheese mixture into the chicken's cuts. Place the chicken breasts in the air fryer basket and top with the remaining cheese.
4. Set the timer for 20 minutes and raise the temperature to 350°F.
5. Serve hot.

Nutritional information

per serving calories: 501 protein: 53.8 g fiber: 0.2 g net carbohydrates: 1.4 g fat: 25.3 g sodium: 860 mg carbohydrates: 1.6 g sugar: 1.0 g

Healthy Air Fryer Chicken and Veggies

Prep Time: 5 minutes
Cook Time: 15 minutes
Total Time: 20 minutes
Servings: 4 servings

Ingredients

- 1 pound chicken breast, chopped into bite-size pieces (2-3 medium chicken breasts)
- 1 cup broccoli florets (fresh or frozen)
- 1 zucchini chopped
- 1 cup bell pepper chopped (any colors you like)
- 1/2 onion chopped
- 2 cloved garlic minced or crushed
- 2 tablespoons olive oil
- 1/2 teaspoon EACH garlic powder, chili powder, salt, pepper
- 1 tablespoon Italian seasoning (or spice blend of choice)

Preparation

1. Turn the air fryer on to 400F.
2. Cut the chicken and vegetables into tiny, bite-sized pieces, then add them to a large mixing bowl.
3. Add the oil and spices to the bowl and toss to mix.
4. Add the chicken and veggies to the preheated air fryer and cook for 10 minutes, shaking midway, or until the chicken and veggies are scorched and poultry is cooked through. You might need to cook them in two or three batches if your air fryer is tiny.

Notes

Spices: Use your preferred spice combination in lieu of the Italian seasoning. Any other mixture—taco, cajun, lemon pepper, etc.—works excellent too! If the mixture already contains salt, just make sure to cut back on it.

Veggies: You may swap out the vegetables with your preferred quick-cooking vegetables. Before using potatoes, air fry them for 10 minutes.

Nutritional information

One serving contains 230 kcal of energy, 8 grams of carbohydrates, 26 grams of protein, 10 grams of fat, 2 grams of saturated fat, and 73 milligrammes of cholesterol. 3g of fibre, 4g of sugar

Teriyaki Wings

Prep Time: 1 hour
Cook Time: 25 minutes
Serves 4

Ingredients

- 2 pounds chicken wings
- 1/2 cup sugar-free teriyaki sauce
- 2 teaspoons minced garlic
- 1/4 teaspoon ground ginger
- 2 teaspoons baking powder

Preparation

1. Put all the ingredients—aside from the baking powder—in a sizable bowl or bag and refrigerate for an hour to marinate.
2. Spread baking powder on the wings before placing them in the air fryer basket. Gently massage the wings.
3. Set the timer for 25 minutes and raise the temperature to 400°F.
4. Toss the basket around a couple of times while cooking.
5. When done, wings should be crispy and have an internal temperature of at least 165°F. Serve right away.

Nutritional information

per serving calories: 446 protein: 41.8 g fiber: 0.1 g net carbohydrates: 3.1 g fat: 29.8 g sodium: 1,034 mg carbohydrates: 3.2 g sugar: 0.0 g

Bang Bang Chicken

Prep time: 15 minutes
cook time: 15 minutes
servings 4

Ingredients

Bang Bang Chicken Sauce
- 1/2 cup mayonnaise
- 2 tablespoons raw honey
- 1/2 tablespoon sriracha sauce or to taste

Bang Bang Chicken Batter
- 1 cup buttermilk
- 2/3 cup all-purpose flour more if needed
- 1/2 cup cornstarch
- 1 egg
- 1 teaspoon sriracha sauce or to taste
- salt and pepper to taste
- 1 lb boneless and skinless chicken breast or chicken thighs - cut into bite size pieces
- 1 cup Panko bread crumbs more in needed
- oil of your choice for greasing air fryer

Preparation

1. In a mixing bowl, combine all the ingredients to make bang bang chicken sauce. Stir everything together using a whisk. Place aside.
2. Produce buttermilk batter by mixing buttermilk, flour, corn starch, egg, sriracha sauce, salt, and pepper in order to make bang bang chicken in an air fryer. then stir everything together.
3. Before adding chicken, grease the air fryer with the oil of your choice. Chicken pieces should then be dipped in buttermilk batter and breadcrumbs before being added to the Air Fryer in batches. Cook chicken in an air fryer at 375°F for 8–10 minutes, or until done. Once on the opposite side, flip the pieces of chicken. (Be careful not to jam too many chicken pieces into the air fryer.
4. Serve the chicken with the sauce over it and a side of fried rice with eggs and green onions or leafy leaves. Enjoy!

Notes

This is a simple chicken dish; for stress-free cooking, have all the ingredients ready and read the directions beforehand.

1 inch chunks of chicken breast should be cut.

To make chicken even more juicy, let the meat sit in a batter in the refrigerator for 30 minutes.

Put leftover bang bang chicken in the refrigerator's airtight container to keep it fresh.

Sriracha sauce can be increased or decreased depending on how hot you prefer your chicken.

Before cooking, grease the air fryer with your preferred oil.

Nutritional information

Serving: 1 g Energy: 601 kcal 53g of carbohydrates, 32g of protein Fat: 28g 6g of saturated fat 14g of polyunsaturated fat 7g of monounsaturated fat 1g of trans fat 132 mg of cholesterol

Chicken Cordon Bleu Casserole

Prep Time: 15 minutes
Cook Time: 15 minutes
Serves 4

Ingredients
- 2 cups cubed cooked chicken thigh meat
- 1/2 cup cubed cooked ham
- 2 ounces Swiss cheese, cubed
- 4 ounces full-fat cream cheese, softened
- 1 tablespoon heavy cream
- 2 tablespoons unsalted butter, melted
- 2 teaspoons Dijon mustard
- 1 ounce pork rinds, crushed

Preparation
1. In a 6" round baking pan, combine the chicken, ham, and cheese; toss to evenly distribute the ingredients.
2. Pour the mixture over the meat and cheese, sprinkle with pork rinds, and place the pan in the air fryer basket. Combine the cream cheese, heavy cream, butter, and mustard in a large bowl.
3. Set the timer for 15 minutes and raise the temperature to 350°F.
4. When finished, the casserole will be bubbling and browned.

Nutritional information
per serving calories: 403 protein: 30.7 g fiber: 0.0 g net carbohydrates: 2.3 g fat: 28.2 g sodium: 660 mg carbohydrates: 2.3 g sugar: 1.2 g

Fajita-Stuffed Chicken Breast

Prep Time: 15 minutes
Cook Time: 25 minutes
Serves 4

Ingredients
- 2 (6-ounce) boneless, skinless chicken breasts
- 1/4 medium white onion, peeled and sliced
- 1 medium green bell pepper, seeded and sliced

- 1 tablespoon coconut oil
- 2 teaspoons chili powder
- 1 teaspoon ground cumin
- 1/2 teaspoon garlic powder

Preparation

1. Each chicken breast should be completely cut in half lengthwise to create two equal pieces. Pound the chicken with a meat tenderizer to a thickness of about 1/4".
2. Each piece of chicken should be laid out, three slices of onion and four slices of green pepper should be placed on the end that is closest to you, and then the chicken should be rolled up tightly with the peppers and onions inside.
3. Place each roll into the air fryer basket, then drizzle coconut oil over the chicken, seasoning each side with chilli powder, cumin, and garlic powder.
4. Set the timer for 25 minutes and raise the temperature to 350°F.
5. Serve hot.

Nutritional information

per serving calories: 146 protein: 19.8 g fiber: 1.2 g net carbohydrates: 2.0 g fat: 4.9 g sodium: 78 mg carbohydrates: 3.2 g sugar: 1.1 g

Broccoli Cheddar Chicken Fritters

Prep Time: 10 minutes
Cook Time: 10 minutes
Servings 8 fritters

Ingredients

- 1 lb boneless skinless chicken thighs, cut into small pieces
- 2 large eggs
- ½ tsp garlic powder
- ½ cup all purpose flour
- 1 cup shredded cheddar cheese
- 2 cups broccoli florets, steamed, and chopped fine
- salt and pepper to taste
- Olive oil

Preparation

1. The bite-sized chicken pieces, garlic powder, eggs, almond flour, shredded cheese, broccoli, salt, and pepper should all be combined in a big dish.
2. gentle blending
3. Scoop the mixture into a GREASED basket using a spoon. In your air fryer, create fritters of the same size. Your air fryer's capacity will determine how many fritters you can make. Put them flat by using the back of a spoon.
4. Cook for 8 minutes at 400°F in your air fryer.
5. Cook for two more minutes after flipping.
6. You may need to fry the fritters for longer if you make them thicker. Before removing from the air fryer, always make sure the food is cooked through.
7. To use up all of your batter, keep performing these steps.

Nutritional information

166kcal of calories, 2g of carbohydrates, 17g of protein, 11g of fat, 1g of fibre, and 1g of sugar.

Chicken Enchiladas

Prep Time: 20 minutes
Cook Time: 10 minutes
Serves 4

Ingredients
- 1 1/2 cups shredded cooked chicken
- 1/3 cup low-carb enchilada sauce, divided
- 1/2 pound medium-sliced deli chicken
- 1 cup shredded medium Cheddar cheese
- 1/2 cup shredded Monterey jack cheese
- 1/2 cup full-fat sour cream
- 1 medium avocado, peeled, pitted, and sliced

Preparation
1. Shredded chicken and half of the enchilada sauce should be combined in a big bowl. On a work surface, arrange slices of deli chicken and spoon 2 tablespoons of the shredded chicken mixture onto each slice.
2. Each roll should receive 2 tablespoons of cheddar. Roll it closed gently.
3. Place each roll seam side down in a 4-cup round baking dish. Cover the rolls with the remaining sauce and Monterey jack. Put the dish in the basket of the air fryer.
4. The timer should be set for 10 minutes with the temperature adjusted to 370°F.
5. When cooked, enchiladas will have a golden top and be bubbling. Serve warm with avocado slices and sour cream.

Nutritional information
per serving calories: 416 protein: 34.2 g fiber: 2.3 g net carbohydrates: 4.2 g fat: 25.2 g sodium: 1,081 mg carbohydrates: 6.5 g sugar: 1.1 g

Pepperoni and Chicken Pizza Bake

Prep Time: 10 minutes
Cook Time: 15 minutes
Serves 4

Ingredients
- 2 cups cubed cooked chicken
- 20 slices pepperoni
- 1 cup low-carb, sugar-free pizza sauce
- 1 cup shredded mozzarella cheese
- 1/4 cup grated Parmesan cheese

Preparation
1. Combine the chicken, pepperoni, and pizza sauce in a 4-cup round baking dish. Meat should be thoroughly coated in sauce after stirring.
2. Add mozzarella and Parmesan cheese on top. Put the dish in the basket of the air fryer.
3. Set the timer for 15 minutes and raise the temperature to 375°F.
4. When cooked, the dish will be bubbling and brown. Serve right away.

Nutritional information
per serving calories: 353 protein: 34.4 g fiber: 1.0 g net carbohydrates: 6.5 g fat: 17.4 g sodium: 754 mg carbohydrates: 7.5 g sugar: 2.3 g

Chicken Patties

Prep Time: 15 minutes
Cook Time: 12 minutes
Serves 4

Ingredients
- 1 pound ground chicken thigh meat
- 1/2 cup shredded mozzarella cheese
- 1 teaspoon dried parsley

- 1/2 teaspoon garlic powder
- 1/4 teaspoon onion powder
- 1 large egg
- 2 ounces pork rinds, finely ground

Preparation
1. Combine the ground chicken, mozzarella, parsley, garlic powder, and onion powder in a sizable bowl. Into four patties, form.
2. When the patties start to firm up, place them in the freezer for 15 to 20 minutes.
3. Egg in a medium bowl, whisking. In a big bowl, add the ground pork rinds.
4. Each chicken patty should be dipped in the egg before being thoroughly coated with pork rinds. Put the air fryer basket with the patties inside.
5. Set the timer for 12 minutes and raise the temperature to 360°F.
6. When finished, patties should be firm and have an internal temperature of 165°F. Serve right away.

Nutritional information

per serving calories: 304 protein: 32.7 g fiber: 0.1 g net carbohydrates: 0.8 g fat: 17.4 g sodium: 406 mg carbohydrates: 0.9 g sugar: 0.2 g

Chicken, Spinach, and Feta Bites

Prep Time: 10 minutes
Cook Time: 12 minutes
Serves 4

Ingredients
- 1 pound ground chicken thigh meat
- 1/3 cup frozen spinach, thawed and drained
- 1/3 cup crumbled feta
- 1/4 teaspoon onion powder
- 1/2 teaspoon garlic powder
- 1/2 ounce pork rinds, finely ground

Preparation
1. In a sizable bowl, combine each ingredient. Working in batches if necessary, roll into 2" balls and place into the air fryer basket.
2. Set the timer for 12 minutes and raise the temperature to 350°F.
3. Serve as soon as possible; internal temperature should be 165°F.

Nutritional information

per serving calories: 220 protein: 24.1 g fiber: 0.4 g net carbohydrates: 1.1 g fat: 12.2 g sodium: 250 mg carbohydrates: 1.5 g sugar: 0.6 g

Greek Chicken Stir-Fry

Prep Time: 15 minutes
Cook Time: 15 minutes
Serves 2

Ingredients

- 1 (6-ounce) chicken breast, cut into 1" cubes
- 1/2 medium zucchini, chopped
- 1/2 medium red bell pepper, seeded and chopped
- 1/4 medium red onion, peeled and sliced
- 1 tablespoon coconut oil
- 1 teaspoon dried oregano
- 1/2 teaspoon garlic powder
- 1/4 teaspoon dried thyme

Preparation

1. Toss everything together in a sizable mixing bowl until the meat and vegetables are coated in coconut oil. Fill the air fryer basket with the bowl's contents.
2. Set the timer for 15 minutes and raise the temperature to 375°F.
3. To distribute the food more evenly during cooking, shake the fryer basket halfway through. Serve right away.

Nutritional information

per serving calories: 186 protein: 20.4 g fiber: 1.7 g net carbohydrates: 3.9 g fat: 8.0 g   sodium: 43 mg carbohydrates: 5.6 g sugar: 3.1 g

Beef Recipes

Air Fryer Steak Bites and Mushrooms

3 Servings
Prep Time: 10 minutes
Cook Time: 18 minutes
Total Time: 28 minutes

Ingredients
- 1 lb. steaks, cut into 1/2" cubes (ribeye, sirloin, tri-tip or what you prefer)
- 8 oz. mushrooms (cleaned, washed and halved)
- 2 Tablespoons Butter, melted (or olive oil)
- 1 teaspoon Worcestershire sauce
- 1/2 teaspoon garlic powder, optional
- flakey salt, to taste
- fresh cracked black pepper, to taste
- Minced parsley, garnish
- Melted butter (for finishing)—optional
- Chili Flakes (for finishing)—optional

Preparation
1. The steak cubes should be well rinsed and dried. Steak cubes and mushrooms should be combined. Add Worcestershire sauce, optional garlic powder, and plenty of salt and pepper after coating with the melted butter.
2. For four minutes, preheat the air fryer to 400°F.
3. In the air fryer basket, put the steak and mushrooms evenly. Avoid packing the basket/tray too full. If necessary, cook in batches.
4. Air fry at 400°F for 6 to 8 minutes. Steak and mushrooms should be shaken and turned. Verify the steak's level of doneness.
5. Add an additional 3-5 minutes to the cooking time, or until the steak is cooked to your satisfaction, if you want it more done (time depends on your preferred doneness, thickness of the steak, size of air fryer).
6. Add optional melted butter, optional chilli flakes, and parsley as garnish. If preferred, season with more salt and pepper. Serve hot.

Nutritional information
401kcal, 3g of carbohydrates, 32g of protein, 29g of fat, 14g of saturated fat, 112mg of cholesterol, 168mg of sodium, 661mg of potassium, and 1g of sugar

Crispy Brats

Prep Time: 5 minutes
Cook Time: 15 minutes
Serves 4

Ingredients
- 4 (3-ounce) beef bratwursts

Preparation
1. Brats should be placed in the air fryer basket.
2. Set the timer for 15 minutes and raise the temperature to 375°F.
3. Serve hot.

Nutritional information
per serving calories: 286 protein: 11.8 g fiber: 0.0 g net carbohydrates: 0.0 g fat: 24.8 g sodium: 50 mg carbohydrates: 0.0 g sugar: 0.0 g

Taco-Stuffed Peppers

Prep Time: 15 minutes
Cook Time: 15 minutes
Serves 4

Ingredients
- 1 pound 80/20 ground beef
- 1 tablespoon chili powder
- 2 teaspoons cumin

- 1 teaspoon garlic powder
- 1 teaspoon salt
- 1/4 teaspoon ground black pepper
- 1 (10-ounce) can diced tomatoes and green chiles, drained
- 4 medium green bell peppers
- 1 cup shredded Monterey jack cheese, divided

Preparation
1. Cook the ground beef in a medium skillet over medium heat for 7 to 10 minutes. Remove the pink from the skillet and drain the fat.
2. Put the skillet back on the heat and season with salt, black pepper, cumin, chilli powder, and garlic powder. Add a drained can of diced tomatoes and some chiles to the skillet. Cook for another three to five minutes.
3. Every bell pepper should be cut in half while the mixture is cooking. Remove the white membrane and seeds. Add a 1/4 cup of cheese on top after evenly distributing the cooked mixture into each bell pepper. Put the air fryer basket with the stuffed peppers inside.
4. Set the timer for 15 minutes and raise the temperature to 350°F.
5. When finished, the cheese will be browned and bubbling, and the peppers will be fork-tender. Serve hot.

Nutritional information
per serving calories: 346 protein: 27.8 g fiber: 3.5 g net carbohydrates: 7.2 g fat: 19.1 g sodium: 991 mg carbohydrates: 10.7 g sugar: 4.9 g

Beef Burrito Bowl

Preparation Time: 5 minutes
Cooking Time: 10 minutes
Servings: 4

Ingredients
- 1 lb. (454 g) 93% lean ground beef
- 1 cup canned low-sodium black beans, drained and rinsed
- 1/4 tsp. ground cumin
- 1/4 tsp. chili powder
- 1/4 tsp. garlic powder
- 1/4 tsp. onion powder
- 1/4 tsp. salt
- 1 head romaine or preferred lettuce, shredded
- 2 medium tomatoes, chopped
- 1 cup shredded Cheddar cheese or packaged cheese blend

Preparation
1. Preheat the air fryer to 400 degrees Fahrenheit.
2. Cook for 8 to 10 minutes, until the meat, beans, cumin, chili powder, garlic powder, onion powder, and salt are cooked thoroughly. Stir seldom.

3. Divide the lettuce into four dishes evenly. Top each bowl with 1/4 of the meat mixture and 1/4 of the tomatoes and cheese.

Nutritional information:
Calories: 351 Fat: 18 g Protein: 35 g Carbs: 14 g Sugars: 4 g Fiber: 6 g Sodium: 424 mg

Classic Mini Meatloaf

Prep Time: 10 minutes
Cook Time: 25 minutes
Serves 6

Ingredients
- 1 pound 80/20 ground beef
- 1/4 medium yellow onion, peeled and diced
- 1/2 medium green bell pepper, seeded and diced
- 1 large egg
- 3 tablespoons blanched finely ground almond flour
- 1 tablespoon Worcestershire sauce
- 1/2 teaspoon garlic powder
- 1 teaspoon dried parsley
- 2 tablespoons tomato paste
- 1/4 cup water
- 1 tablespoon powdered erythritol

Preparation
1. Ground beef, onion, pepper, egg, and almond flour should all be combined in a big bowl. Add the Worcestershire sauce, parsley, and garlic powder to the bowl. Completely combine by blending.
2. Place the mixture into two (4") loaf baking pans after dividing it in half.
3. Combine the tomato paste, water, and erythritol in a small bowl. Each loaf should receive half the mixture.
4. If necessary, add loaf pans to the air fryer basket in batches.
5. Set the temperature to 350°F and cook for 25 minutes, or until the internal temperature reaches 180°F.
6. Serve hot.

Nutritional information
per serving calories: 170 protein: 14.9 g fiber: 0.9 g net carbohydrates: 2.6 g sugar alcohol: 1.5 g fat: 9.4 g sodium: 85 mg carbohydrates: 5.0 g sugar: 1.5 g

Chorizo and Beef Burger

Prep Time: 10 minutes
Cook Time: 15 minutes
Serves 4

Ingredients
- 3/4 pound 80/20 ground beef
- 1/4 pound Mexican-style ground chorizo
- 1/4 cup chopped onion
- 5 slices pickled jalapeños, chopped
- 2 teaspoons chili powder
- 1 teaspoon minced garlic
- 1/4 teaspoon cumin

Preparation
1. Combine all ingredients in a sizable bowl. Burger patties are created by dividing the mixture into four equal portions.
2. Working in batches if necessary, place the burger patties into the air fryer basket.
3. Set the timer for 15 minutes and raise the temperature to 375°F.
4. Halfway through the cooking process, flip the patties. Serve hot.

Nutritional information
per serving calories: 291 protein: 21.6 g fiber: 0.9 g net carbohydrates: 3.8 g fat: 18.3 g sodium: 474 mg carbohydrates: 4.7 g sugar: 2.5 g

Bacon Cheeseburger Casserole

Prep Time: 15 minutes
Cook Time: 20 minutes
Serves 4

Ingredients
- 1 pound ground beef
- 1/4 medium white onion, peeled and chopped
- 1 cup shredded Cheddar cheese, divided
- 1 large egg
- 4 slices sugar-free bacon, cooked and crumbled
- 2 pickle spears, chopped

Preparation
1. In a medium skillet over medium heat, brown the ground beef for about 7 to 10 minutes. Drain the fat once there is no pink left. Add ground beef to a sizable mixing bowl after removing from the heat.
2. Add egg, onion, and half a cup of Cheddar to the bowl. Add the bacon crumbles after thoroughly combining the ingredients.
3. Place the remaining Cheddar on top of the mixture before adding it to a 4-cup round baking dish. Place in the basket of the air fryer.
4. Set the timer for 20 minutes and raise the temperature to 375°F.
5. When a casserole is fully cooked, the top will be golden and the centre will be firm. Serve right away with pickles chopped on top.

Nutritional information
per serving calories: 369 protein: 31.0 g fiber: 0.2 g net carbohydrates: 1.0 g fat: 22.6 g sodium: 454 mg carbohydrates: 1.2 g sugar: 0.5 g

Peppercorn-Crusted Beef Tenderloin

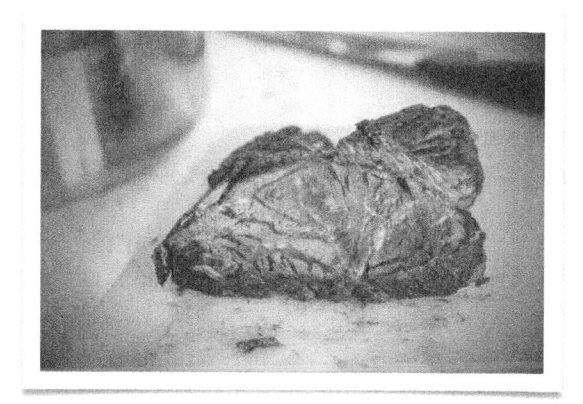

Prep Time: 10 minutes
Cook Time: 25 minutes
Serves 6

Ingredients
- 2 tablespoons salted butter, melted
- 2 teaspoons minced roasted garlic
- 3 tablespoons ground 4-peppercorn blend
- 1 (2-pound) beef tenderloin, trimmed of visible fat

Preparation
1. Combine the butter and roasted garlic in a small bowl. Over the beef tenderloin, brush it.
2. Roll the tenderloin through the ground peppercorns on a plate to form a crust. Tenderloin should be placed in the air fryer basket.
3. Set the timer for 25 minutes and raise the temperature to 400°F.
4. About halfway through the cooking process, turn the tenderloin.
5. Before slicing, give the meat 10 minutes to rest.

Nutritional information
per serving calories: 289 protein: 34.7 g fiber: 0.9 g net carbohydrates: 1.6 g fat: 13.8 g sodium: 96 mg carbohydrates: 2.5 g sugar: 0.0 g

Easy Lasagna Casserole

Prep Time: 15 minutes
Cook Time: 15 minutes
Serves 4

Ingredients
- 3/4 cup low-carb no-sugar-added pasta sauce
- 1 pound 80/20 ground beef, cooked and drained
- 1/2 cup full-fat ricotta cheese

- 1/4 cup grated Parmesan cheese
- 1/2 teaspoon garlic powder
- 1 teaspoon dried parsley
- 1/2 teaspoon dried oregano
- 1 cup shredded mozzarella cheese

Preparation

1. Pour 1/4 cup pasta sauce into the bottom of a 4-cup round baking dish. Lay out a quarter of the ground beef over the sauce.
2. Ricotta, Parmesan, garlic salt, parsley, and oregano should all be combined in a small bowl. Dollop the beef with the remaining half of the mixture.
3. Add a third of the mozzarella. Continue layering until all of the beef, ricotta mixture, sauce, and mozzarella have been used; top with mozzarella.
4. Place the dish in the air fryer basket after covering it with foil.
5. The timer should be set for 15 minutes with the temperature adjusted to 370°F.
6. Remove the foil for the final two minutes of cooking so the cheese can brown. Serve right away.

Nutritional information

per serving calories: 371 protein: 31.4 g fiber: 1.6 g net carbohydrates: 4.2 g fat: 21.4 g sodium: 633 mg carbohydrates: 5.8 g sugar: 1.9 g

Ground Beef Taco Rolls

Prep Time: 20 minutes
Cook Time: 10 minutes
Serves 4

Ingredients

- 1/2 pound ground beef
- 1/3 cup water
- 1 tablespoon chili powder
- 2 teaspoons cumin
- 1/2 teaspoon garlic powder
- 1/4 cup canned diced tomatoes and chiles, drained
- 2 tablespoons chopped cilantro
- 1 1/2 cups shredded mozzarella cheese
- 1/2 cup blanched finely ground almond flour
- 2 ounces full-fat cream cheese
- 1 large egg

Preparation

1. Cook the ground beef in a medium skillet over medium heat for 7 to 10 minutes. Drain meat once it has finished cooking.
2. Stir in tomatoes with chiles, cumin, chilli powder, garlic powder, and oregano after adding water to the skillet. Include cilantro. After bringing to a boil, turn heat down to a simmer for three minutes.
3. Place the mozzarella, almond flour, cream cheese, and egg in a sizable microwave-safe bowl. Place in a microwave for one minute.

Rapidly stir the mixture until a smooth dough ball forms.
4. Create a work surface for yourself out of parchment. On the parchment, shape the dough into a large rectangle by pressing it down while occasionally moistening your hands to keep it from sticking. Create eight rectangles out of the dough.
5. Put a few spoonfuls of the meat mixture on each rectangle. Each roll should be folded with the short ends toward the centre and rolled lengthwise like a burrito.
6. Cut a piece of parchment to fit the basket of your air fryer. Taco rolls should be placed on the parchment and then into the basket of the air fryer.
7. Set the timer for 10 minutes and raise the temperature to 360°F.
8. Halfway through the cooking process, flip.
9. 10 minutes should pass before serving.

Nutritional information

per serving calories: 380 protein: 24.8 g fiber: 2.5 g net carbohydrates: 4.5 g fat: 26.5 g sodium: 452 mg carbohydrates: 7.0 g sugar: 2.0 g

Air Fryer Steak With Garlic-Herb Butter

Total: 30 minutes
Active: 10 minutes
Yield: 2 servings

Ingredients
- One inch-thick, one-pound sirloin steak, kosher salt, and freshly ground black pepper
- Unsalted butter, 4 tablespoons, at room temperature
- 1 tablespoon of fresh parsley, cut very finely
- 1 tablespoon fresh chives, chopped finely
- 1 little clove of grated garlic
- 1/4 teaspoon of red pepper flakes, crushed

Preparation
1. Before cooking, let the steak rest at room temperature for 30 minutes.
2. Air fryer needs should be set to 400 degrees Fahrenheit. some grinds of black pepper and a hefty teaspoon of salt should be used to season the steak on both sides. For medium-rare, medium, and medium-well doneness, place the steak in the centre of the air fryer basket and cook for about 10 minutes, 12 minutes, and 14 minutes, respectively. After moving the steak to a chopping board, give it 10 minutes to rest.
3. In the meantime, mix the butter, parsley, chives, garlic, and red pepper flakes in a small bowl. Cut the steak into 1/4-inch-thick slices by cutting it against the grain. Add the garlic-herb butter on top.

Air-Fried Pizza Burgers

Prep Time 10 minutes
Cook Time 15 minutes
Total Time 25 minutes
Servings: 4

Ingredients

- 1 pound meatloaf mix ground beef, veal and pork
- 1 tablespoon minced onion
- 1/3 cup chopped pepperoni or mini pepperoni slices
- 1 tablespoon tomato paste
- 1 teaspoon Italian seasoning
- 1/2 teaspoon salt
- freshly ground black pepper
- 1 cup pizza sauce
- 6 ounces sliced mozzarella cheese
- 4 crusty round rolls ciabatta rolls or focaccia bread

Preparation

1. In a large bowl, combine the meatloaf mixture, finely chopped onion, pepperoni, tomato paste, Italian seasoning, salt, and pepper. Mix well until everything is mixed. Without overhandling the meat, divide the meat into 4 equal halves, and then assemble the hamburgers. Throwing the meat between your hands like a baseball and packing it each time you catch it is a nice method for doing this. Create a divot or depression in the centre of each burger by flattening the balls into patties. As it cooks, this will assist in keeping the burger flat.
2. Sliced the rolls in half, then lightly drizzle the cut side with olive oil.
3. Set the air fryer to 370°F in advance.
4. The burger patties should be air-fried for 15 minutes, turning them over halfway through. Each burger should have some pizza sauce on it before being topped with sliced mozzarella cheese. 3 additional minutes of air-frying at 370°F are required to melt the cheese.
5. The burgers should be taken out of the air fryer and let to rest. Place the rolls in the air fryer, cut side up. To toast the rolls, air-fry them for 2 to 3 minutes at 380°F.
6. Place the burgers on the toasted buns when they have rested, cover with extra Italian spice, and serve right away.

Nutritional information

Amount Per Serving 534 Calories Fat 28g Saturated Fat 11g Cholesterol 116mg Sodium 1426mg Potassium 305mg Carbohydrates 32g Fiber 1g Sugar 3g Protein 43g

Oversized BBQ Meatballs

Prep Time: 10 minutes
Cook Time: 14 minutes
Serves 4

Ingredients
- 1 pound 80/20 ground beef
- 1/4 pound ground Italian sausage
- 1 large egg
- 1/4 teaspoon onion powder
- 1/2 teaspoon garlic powder
- 1 teaspoon dried parsley
- 4 slices sugar-free bacon, cooked and chopped
- 1/4 cup chopped white onion
- 1/4 cup chopped pickled jalapeños
- 1/2 cup low-carb, sugar-free barbecue sauce

Preparation
1. Mix the ground beef, sausage, and egg thoroughly in a big bowl. Including barbecue sauce last, combine all other ingredients. Eight meatballs should be formed. Put the meatballs in the basket of the air fryer.
2. Set the timer for 14 minutes and raise the temperature to 400°F.
3. About halfway through the cooking process, turn the meatballs.
4. Meatballs should be cooked through and have an internal temperature of at least 180°F when they are finished.
5. Take the meatballs out of the fryer and mix with the barbecue sauce. Serve hot.

Nutritional information
per serving calories: 336 protein: 28.1 g fiber: 0.4 g net carbohydrates: 4.0 g fat: 19.5 g sodium: 761 mg carbohydrates: 4.4 g sugar: 0.7 g

Empanadas

Prep Time: 15 minutes
Cook Time: 10 minutes
Yields 4 empanadas (1 per serving)

Ingredients

- 1 pound 80/20 ground beef
- 1/4 cup water
- 1/4 cup diced onion
- 2 teaspoons chili powder
- 1/2 teaspoon garlic powder
- 1/4 teaspoon cumin
- 1 1/2 cups shredded mozzarella cheese
- 1/2 cup blanched finely ground almond flour
- 2 ounces full-fat cream cheese
- 1 large egg

Preparation

1. Cook the ground beef in a medium skillet over medium heat for 7 to 10 minutes. Remove the fat. Stove the skillet back on.
2. Add onion and water to the skillet. Cumin, garlic, and chilli powder are added after stirring. Simmer for an additional three to five minutes on low heat. When heat has been removed; set aside.
3. Add cream cheese, mozzarella, and almond flour to a sizable microwave-safe bowl. Heat one minute in a microwave until smooth; stir. Form a ball out of the mixture.
4. Cut the dough into four squares. Place 1/4 of the ground beef on the bottom half of each square. Fold the dough over and roll the edges up or press with a wet fork to seal. Place the dough between two sheets of parchment paper and roll out to a thickness of 1/4".
5. Brush egg over empanadas by cracking it into a small bowl and whisking it.
6. Place the empanadas on a piece of parchment that has been cut to fit your air fryer basket and put the parchment into the air fryer basket.
7. Set the timer for 10 minutes and raise the temperature to 400°F.
8. Serve the empanadas warm after flipping them halfway through cooking.

Nutritional information

per serving calories: 463 protein: 33.3 g fiber: 2.2 g net carbohydrates: 4.3 g fat: 30.8 g sodium: 426 mg carbohydrates: 6.5 g sugar: 1.9 g

Reverse Seared Ribeye

Prep Time: 5 minutes
Cook Time: 45 minutes
Serves 2

Ingredients
- 1 (8-ounce) ribeye steak
- 1/2 teaspoon pink Himalayan salt
- 1/4 teaspoon ground peppercorn
- 1 tablespoon coconut oil
- 1 tablespoon salted butter, softened
- 1/4 teaspoon garlic powder
- 1/2 teaspoon dried parsley
- 1/4 teaspoon dried oregano

Preparation
1. Season steak with salt and freshly ground pepper. Place in the basket of the air fryer.
2. Set the timer for 45 minutes and raise the temperature to 250°F.
3. Once the timer has beeped, start checking for doneness and keep adding minutes until the internal temperature is as you like it.
4. Add coconut oil to a medium skillet set over medium heat. Quickly sear the outside and sides of the steak in the hot oil until they are crisp and browned. Steak should rest after being taken off the heat.
5. Combine butter, oregano, parsley, and garlic powder in a small bowl.
6. Steak should be served sliced with herb butter on top.

Nutritional information
per serving calories: 377 protein: 22.6 g fiber: 0.2 g net carbohydrates: 0.4 g fat: 30.7 g sodium: 490 mg carbohydrates: 0.6 g sugar: 0.0 g

Pub-Style Burger

Prep Time: 10 minutes
Cook Time: 10 minutes
Serves 4

Ingredients
- 1 pound ground sirloin
- 1/2 teaspoon salt
- 1/4 teaspoon ground black pepper
- 2 tablespoons salted butter, melted
- 1/2 cup full-fat mayonnaise
- 2 teaspoons sriracha
- 1/4 teaspoon garlic powder
- 8 large leaves butter lettuce
- 4 Bacon-Wrapped Onion Rings (Chapter 3)
- 8 slices pickle

Preparation
1. Mix ground sirloin, salt, and pepper in a medium bowl. assemble four patties. Place each into the air fryer basket after being butter-brushed.
2. The timer should be set for 10 minutes with the temperature adjusted to 380°F.
3. For a medium burger, flip the patties halfway through cooking. For well-done, add an additional 3–5 minutes.
4. Combine mayonnaise, sriracha, and garlic powder in a small bowl. Place aside.
5. Each cooked burger should be placed on a lettuce leaf along with an onion ring, two pickles, and a dollop of the burger sauce you have made. To hold, tightly wrap another lettuce leaf around. Serve hot.

Nutritional information
per serving calories: 442 protein: 22.3 g fiber: 0.8 g net carbohydrates: 3.3 g fat: 34.9 g sodium: 928 mg carbohydrates: 4.1 g sugar: 2.3 g

Fajita Flank Steak Rolls

Prep Time: 20 minutes
Cook Time: 15 minutes
Serves 6

Ingredients
- 2 tablespoons unsalted butter
- 1/4 cup diced yellow onion
- 1 medium red bell pepper, seeded and sliced into strips
- 1 medium green bell pepper, seeded and sliced into strips
- 2 teaspoons chili powder
- 1 teaspoon cumin
- 1/2 teaspoon garlic powder
- 2 pounds flank steak
- 4 (1-ounce) slices pepper jack cheese

Preparation
1. Butter should be melted in a medium skillet over medium heat before onion, red bell pepper, and green bell pepper are started to be sautéed. Add a dash of garlic, cumin, and chilli powder. About 5-7 minutes of sautéing should make the peppers tender.
2. Place the flank steak flat on a work surface. Cover the entire rectangle of steak with the onion and pepper mixture. Nearly overlapping cheese slices should be placed over the onions and peppers.
3. Start rolling the steak with the shorter end facing you, tucking the cheese into the roll as necessary. Twelve toothpicks, six on each side of the steak roll, are used to secure it. Put the air fryer basket with the steak roll inside.
4. Set the timer for 15 minutes and raise the temperature to 400°F.
5. Halfway through the cooking process, rotate the roll. Depending on your preferred internal temperature (135°F for medium), add an additional 1-4 minutes.
6. After the timer beeps, slice the roll into six equal pieces and let it rest for 15 minutes. Serve hot.

Nutritional information
per serving calories: 439 protein: 38.0 g fiber: 1.2 g net carbohydrates: 2.5 g fat: 26.6 g sodium: 226 mg carbohydrates: 3.7 g sugar: 1.8 g

Air Fryer Juicy Steak Bites

Prep Time: 7 minutes
Cook Time: 12 minutes
Total Time: 19 minutes
Servings: 3 servings

Ingredients

- 2 lb sirloin steak (cut into 1½-inch by 1-inch)
- 2 tbsp oil
- 1½ tsp ground black pepper
- 1½ tsp salt
- 1½ tsp soy sauce

Preparation

1. Slice the meat into 112 by 1 inch pieces.
2. Oil, pepper, salt, and soy sauce are all whisked together.
3. In a bowl, place the steak and mix with the sauce to coat.
4. Heat the air fryer.
5. Cook for 7–12 minutes in an air fryer at 400°F.
6. 12 minutes for medium-well, 7 minutes for more rare.
7. Serve as a main meal with noodles, steaming rice, and veggies.

Notes

Flavor Variations

- Onions: Before heating, add some diced white or yellow onions to the sauce in your dish and stir thoroughly.
- Mushrooms: Mushrooms go well with steak. Simply add the mushrooms to the dish, add a little extra oil to cover them in the sauce, and air fried them with the steak pieces.
- Garlic, ginger, paprika, cumin, coriander, chilli powder, lemon juice, and toasted sesame seeds are other spices that pair well with soy sauce.
- Serving suggestions for the sauces include chimichurri, hummus, tzatziki, A1 sauce, barbecue sauce, mustard cream, butter garlic sauce, steak Diane sauce, Worcestershire sauce, and Cajun butter sauce.
- Blue cheese crumbles are my absolute favourite topping on steak. When the steak has finished cooking, add some crumbled blue cheese and let it meld a little with the flesh. This option is now available at several well-known steakhouses, and I truly appreciate it. It gives the meat an acidic, biting flavour.
- When the air fryer steak is finished frying, place it in a bowl with some butter. This component will provide the dish taste in addition to moisture.
- Garlic: If marinating, add the garlic at the start to seal in even more garlic flavour. Then, prepare the food as directed in the recipe. When serving the meat for supper, mince the garlic and combine it with a little melted butter if you like raw garlic as I do.

Nutritional information

495 kcal of calories, 1 g of carbohydrate, 66 g of protein, 23 g of fat, 6 g of saturated fat, 3 g of polyunsaturated fat, 12 g of monounsaturated fat, 1 g of trans fat, 1 g of fibre, and 1 g of sugar.

Air Fryer Beef and Bean Chimichangas

Prep Time 15 minutes
Cook Time 8 minutes
Total Time 23 minutes
Servings 10
Calories 580 Kcal

Ingredients
- 1 Pound Ground Beef
- 1 Package Taco Seasoning
- 1/2 Cup Refried Beans
- 1/2 Cup Shredded Colby Jack Cheese
- 10 Taco Size Flour Tortillas or 5 Burrito Flour Size Tortillas
- Toppings - Queso Lettuce, Tomato, Sour Cream, Salsa

Preparation
1. As directed, brown the ground beef and add the taco spice. You may carry out this action utilising the saute setting on a Ninja Foodi.
2. Add the refried beans once the meat has finished cooking.
3. Each tortilla should have the filling in the centre, followed by shredded cheese.
4. To ensure that all of the toppings are firmly within the tortilla, fold it up.
5. Apply nonstick cooking spray or olive oil spray to the air fryer.
6. Put the chimichangas in the air fryer seam side down.
7. Apply a layer of olive oil spray on them. Cooking spray made from avocados may also be used for this.
8. Cook for 8 minutes at 360 degrees. To ensure they are cooked properly, check on them after 5 minutes.
9. Once finished, the tortilla should be snugly wrapped and just just browned on top.

Nutritional information
Serving: 1 g Energy: 580 kcal 66g of carbohydrates 29g of protein Fat: 22g 9g of saturated fat 11g of polyunsaturated fat 1g of trans fat 63mg of cholesterol Salt: 986 mg 7g of fibre 4g sugar

Meatloaf Slider Wraps

Prep Time: 15 minutes
Cook Time: 10 minutes
Servings: 2

Ingredients

- 1 pound ground beef, grass-fed
- 1/2 cup almond flour
- 1/4 cup coconut flour
- 1/2 tbsp. minced garlic
- 1/4 cup chopped white onion
- 1 tsp. Italian seasoning
- 1/2 tsp. sea salt
- 1/2 tsp. dried tarragon
- 1/2 tsp. ground black pepper
- 1 tbsp. Worcestershire sauce
- 1/4 cup ketchup
- 2 eggs, pastured, beaten
- 1 head of lettuce

Preparation

1. In a mixing bowl, combine all of the ingredients and toss well. Shape the mixture into 2-inch diameter and 1-inch thick patties and chill for 10 minutes.
2. Meanwhile, turn on the air fryer, insert the frying basket, coat it with olive oil, close the cover, and warm for 10 minutes at 360°F.
3. Open the fryer, place the patties in a single layer, shut the lid, and cook for 10 minutes, or until pleasantly browned and done, flipping midway through the cooking.
4. When the air fryer sounds, remove the patties and place them on a platter.
5. Wrap each burger with lettuce before serving.

Nutritional information

Calories: 228 Carbs: 6 g Fat: 16 g Protein: 13 g Fiber: 2 g

Pork Recipes

Pork Rind Nachos

Prep Time: 5 minutes
Cook Time: 5 minutes
Serves 2

Ingredients
- 1 ounce pork rinds
- 4 ounces shredded cooked chicken
- 1/2 cup shredded Monterey jack cheese
- 1/4 cup sliced pickled jalapeños
- 1/4 cup guacamole
- 1/4 cup full-fat sour cream

Preparation
1. Pork rinds should be placed in a 6" round baking pan. Shredded chicken and Monterey jack cheese should be added.
2. Set the temperature to 370 degrees Fahrenheit, and then set the timer for 5 minutes, or until the cheese is melted.
3. Serve immediately after adding the jalapenos, guacamole, and sour cream on top.

Nutritional information
per serving calories: 395 protein: 30.1 g fiber: 1.2 g net carbohydrates: 1.8 g fat: 27.5 g sodium: 763 mg carbohydrates: 3.0 g sugar: 1.0 g

Crispy Pork Chop Salad

Prep Time: 15 minutes
Cook Time: 8 minutes
Serves 2

Ingredients

- 1 tablespoon coconut oil
- 2 (4-ounce) pork chops, chopped into 1" cubes
- 2 teaspoons chili powder
- 1 teaspoon paprika
- 1/2 teaspoon garlic powder
- 1/4 teaspoon onion powder
- 4 cups chopped romaine
- 1 medium Roma tomato, diced
- 1/2 cup shredded Monterey jack cheese
- 1 medium avocado, peeled, pitted, and diced
- 1/4 cup full-fat ranch dressing
- 1 tablespoon chopped cilantro

Preparation

1. Put the pork in a big bowl and cover it with coconut oil. Chili powder, paprika, garlic powder, and onion powder should be added. Pork should be placed in the air fryer basket.
2. Set the timer for 8 minutes and raise the temperature to 400°F.
3. When fully cooked, pork will be golden and crispy.
4. Put romaine, tomato, and crispy pork in a big bowl. Add avocado and cheese to the top. Toss the salad with the ranch dressing in the bowl to coat it completely.
5. Adding cilantro last. Serve right away.

Nutritional information

per serving calories: 526 protein: 34.4 g fiber: 8.6 g net carbohydrates: 5.2 g fat: 37.0 g sodium: 354 mg carbohydrates: 13.8 g sugar: 3.1 g

Breaded Pork Chops

Prep Time: 10 minutes
Cook Time: 15 minutes
Serves 4

Ingredients
- 1 1/2 ounces pork rinds, finely ground
- 1 teaspoon chili powder
- 1/2 teaspoon garlic powder
- 1 tablespoon coconut oil, melted
- 4 (4-ounce) pork chops

Preparation
1. Combine ground pork rinds, chilli powder, and garlic powder in a sizable bowl.
2. Each pork chop should be brushed with coconut oil before being pressed into the pork rind mixture to coat both sides. Put the air fryer basket with each coated pork chop inside.
3. Set the timer for 15 minutes and raise the temperature to 400°F.
4. Each pork chop is turned over halfway through cooking.
5. The pork chops should be at least 145°F internally and have a golden exterior when fully cooked.

Nutritional information
per serving calories: 292 protein: 29.5 g fiber: 0.3 g net carbohydrates: 0.3 g fat: 18.5 g sodium: 268 mg carbohydrates: 0.6 g sugar: 0.1 g

Easy Juicy Pork Chops

Prep Time: 5 minutes
Cook Time: 15 minutes
Serves 2

Ingredients
- 1 teaspoon chili powder
- 1/2 teaspoon garlic powder
- 1/2 teaspoon cumin
- 1/4 teaspoon ground black pepper
- 1/4 teaspoon dried oregano
- 2 (4-ounce) boneless pork chops
- 2 tablespoons unsalted butter, divided

Preparation
1. Combine the chilli powder, garlic powder, cumin, pepper, and oregano in a small bowl. On the pork chops, apply a dry rub. Pork chops should be placed in the air fryer basket.
2. Set the timer for 15 minutes and raise the temperature to 400°F.
3. When fully cooked, the internal temperature should be at least 145°F. Serve each warm with 1 tablespoon of butter on top.

Nutritional information

per serving calories: 313 protein: 24.4 g fiber: 0.7 g net carbohydrates: 1.1 g fat: 22.6 g sodium: 117 mg carbohydrates: 1.8 g sugar: 0.1 g

Pulled Pork

Prep Time: 10 minutes
Cook Time: 2 1/2 hours
Serves 8

Ingredients
- 2 tablespoons chili powder
- 1 teaspoon garlic powder
- 1/2 teaspoon onion powder
- 1/2 teaspoon ground black pepper
- 1/2 teaspoon cumin
- 1 (4-pound) pork shoulder

Preparation
1. Combine the chilli powder, cumin, pepper, garlic, and onion powders in a small bowl. The skin of the pork shoulder should be covered with the spice mixture as you rub it in. Put the air fryer basket with the pork shoulder inside.
2. Set the thermostat to 350 degrees Fahrenheit and the timer to 150 minutes.
3. When done, the meat can be easily shredded with two forks and the skin will be crispy. At least 145°F should be present internally.

Nutritional information

per serving calories: 537 protein: 42.6 g fiber: 0.8 g net carbohydrates: 0.7 g fat: 35.5 g sodium: 180 mg carbohydrates: 1.5 g sugar: 0.2 g

Italian Stuffed Bell Peppers

Prep Time: 15 minutes
Cook Time: 15 minutes
Serves 4

Ingredients

- 1 pound ground pork Italian sausage
- 1/2 teaspoon garlic powder
- 1/2 teaspoon dried parsley
- 1 medium Roma tomato, diced
- 1/4 cup chopped onion
- 4 medium green bell peppers
- 1 cup shredded mozzarella cheese, divided

Preparation

1. Cook the ground sausage in a medium skillet over medium heat for 7 to 10 minutes or until no pink is visible. The skillet's fat should be drained.
2. Put the skillet back on the heat and add the tomato, onion, tomato powder, and parsley. Cook for another three to five minutes.
3. Remove the seeds and white membrane from peppers by cutting them in half.
4. Spoon the meat mixture evenly into the pepper halves after removing it from the stove. Add mozzarella on top. Put the air fryer basket with the pepper halves inside.
5. Set the timer for 15 minutes and raise the temperature to 350°F.
6. When finished, cheese will be golden and peppers fork-tender. Serve hot.

Nutritional information

per serving calories: 358 protein: 21.1 g fiber: 2.6 g net carbohydrates: 8.7 g fat: 24.1 g sodium: 1,029 mg carbohydrates: 11.3 g sugar: 4.8 g

Air Fryer Pork Chops and Broccoli

Yield 2 Servings
Prep Time: 5 Minutes
Cook Time: 10 Minutes
Total Time: 15 Minutes

Ingredients

- 2 5 ounce bone-in pork chops
- 2 tablespoons avocado oil, divided
- 1/2 teaspoon paprika
- 1/2 teaspoon onion powder
- 1/2 teaspoon garlic powder
- 1 teaspoon salt, divided
- 2 cups broccoli florets
- 2 cloves garlic, minced

Preparation

1. As directed by the manufacturer, preheat the air fryer to 350 degrees. Spray some nonstick spray on the basket.
2. The pork chops should have 1 tablespoon of oil on both sides.
3. With the paprika, onion powder, garlic powder, and 1/2 teaspoon salt, season the pork chops on both sides.
4. Cook pork chops for 5 minutes in the air fryer basket.
5. The broccoli, garlic, last 1/2 teaspoon of salt, and last tablespoon of oil are added to a bowl and mixed together while the pork chops are cooking.
6. Flip the pork chops in the air fryer slowly.
7. Return the basket to the air fryer and add the broccoli.
8. After the additional five minutes, stir the broccoli once.
9. Serve the dish after carefully removing it from the air fryer.

Notes

For this dish, preheat the oven to 375 degrees and bake the broccoli for 30 minutes, tossing the broccoli every ten minutes.

Pork chops that were about half an inch thick were utilised. Adjust cook times if using pork chops that are thicker or thinner.

If you're going to double this recipe to feed a family of four, I suggest frying all four pork chops at once (provided your air fryer has enough space for them), moving them to a platter, and then covering them completely with foil while the broccoli cooks.

Nutrition information

483 calories 30g total fat 7g of saturated fat 0g of trans fat 20g of unsaturated fat 119 mg of cholesterol 1201 mg of sodium 12g of carbohydrates 6g of net carbohydrates 6g of fibre 2g sugar 40g of protein

Keto Air Fryer Pork Belly Bites

Prep Time: 5 minutes
Cook Time: 15 minutes
Total Time: 20 minutes
Servings 4 People

Ingredients

- ½ pound pork belly
- 2 tablespoon olive oil
- 1 tablespoon swerve brown sugar
- 1 teaspoon garlic powder
- ¼ teaspoon black pepper
- 1 teaspoon Chili Pepper Flakes

Preparation

1. Heat air fryer to 400°F.
2. Slice the pork belly into bite-sized pieces, then combine with the remaining ingredients in a bowl and toss to combine.
3. If necessary, use cooking spray to coat the air fryer basket before adding the pork belly, making sure to leave space between each piece.
4. Flip or shake the basket every five minutes while air frying for 15-20 minutes. Cook to the desired level of crispness.

Nutritional information

Amount per Serving Calories 236 Fat 22g Carbohydrates 1g Fiber 0 g Sugar 0 g Protein 10 g

Lemon and Honey Pork Tenderloin

Preparation Time: 5 minutes
Cooking Time: 10 minutes
Servings: 4

Ingredients
- 1 (1 pound/454 g) pork tenderloin, cut into ½-inch slices
- 1 tbsp. olive oil
- 1 tbsp. freshly squeezed lemon juice
- 1 tbsp. honey
- 1/2 tsp. grated lemon zest
- 1/2 tsp. dried marjoram
- Pinch salt Freshly ground black pepper to taste

Preparation
1. In a medium mixing dish, combine the pork tenderloin pieces.
2. Combine the olive oil, lemon juice, honey, lemon zest, marjoram, salt, and pepper in a small bowl. Mix.
3. Pour the marinade over the tenderloin slices and rub it in lightly with your hands.
4. Place the pork in the air fryer basket and heat at 400°F for 10 minutes, or until a meat thermometer reads at least 145°F.

Nutritional information
Calories: 208 Fat: 8 g Protein: 30 g Carbs: 5 g Fiber: 0 g Sugar: 4 g Sodium: 104 mg

Pork Burgers With Red Cabbage Slaw

Preparation Time: 20 minutes
Cooking Time: 7-9 minutes
Servings: 4

Ingredients
- 1/2 cup Greek yogurt
- 2 tbsp. low-sodium mustard, divided

- 1 tbsp. freshly squeezed lemon juice
- 1/4 cup sliced red cabbage
- 1/4 cup grated carrots
- 1 pound (454 g) lean ground pork
- 1/2 tsp. paprika
- 1 cup mixed baby lettuce greens
- 2 small tomatoes, sliced
- 8 small low-sodium whole-wheat sandwich buns, cut in half

Preparation
1. Refrigerate the yogurt, 1 tablespoon mustard, lemon juice, cabbage, and carrots in a small dish.
2. Combine the pork, the remaining 1 tablespoon mustard, and the paprika in a medium mixing basin. Make 8 tiny patties.
3. Place the patties in an air fryer basket. Air fry for 7 to 9 minutes at 400°F or until the patties register 165°F when measured with a meat thermometer.
4. Assemble the burgers by laying some lettuce greens on the bottom of the buns. Finish with a tomato slice, patties, and cabbage mixture. Serve immediately with the bun top.

Nutritional information
Calories: 473 Fat: 15 g Protein: 35 g Carbs: 51 g Fiber: 8 g Sugar: 8 g Sodium: 138 mg

Pork Taquitos in Air Fryer

Preparation Time: 10 minutes
Cooking Time: 7-10 minutes
Servings: 2

Ingredients
- 3 cups pork tenderloin, cooked and shredded Cooking spray
- 2 ½ shredded mozzarella, fat-free
- 10 small tortillas
- 1 lime juice

Preparation
1. Preheat the air fryer to 380°F.
2. Mix in the lime juice with the meat.
3. Microwave for 10 seconds with a moist cloth over the tortilla to soften.
4. Place the pork filling and cheese on top of a tortilla and roll it up tightly.
5. Place the tortillas on a foil-lined baking sheet.
6. Spray the tortillas with oil. Cook for 7 to 10 minutes, or until golden brown, flipping halfway through.
7. Serve alongside a nice salad.

Nutritional information
Calories: 253 Fat: 18 g Carbs: 10 g Protein: 20 g

Lamb Recipes

Garlic Sauce and Lamb Chops

Servings 4 people
Preparation time: 15 minutes,
Cooking time: 22 minutes

Ingredients

- 1 bulb of garlic
- 3 tablespoons of olive oil
- 1 tbsp fresh oregano, finely chopped
- sea-salt
- Freshly ground black pepper
- 8 lamb chops

Preparation

1. Preheat the air fryer to 392° F. Brush the garlic bulb with olive oil and place it in the basket. Set the timer for 12 minutes and place the basket in the airfryer. Bake the garlic until it is soft.
2. Meanwhile, combine the herbs with a pinch of sea salt, pepper, and olive oil. Brush the lamb chops with half a spoonful of the herbal oil and let aside for 5 minutes.
3. Preheat the air fryer at 392° F. and remove the garlic bulb from the basket.
4. Place four lamb chops in the basket and place it in the air fryer. Set your timer for 5 minutes. Brown the lamb chops in a skillet. They can still be crimson or pink on the inside. Keep heated in a pan while you cook the remaining lamb chops.
5. With the garlic sauce, serve the lamb chops. It goes well with couscous and cooked zucchini.

Greek Lamb Pita Pockets

Preparation Time: 15 minutes
Cooking Time: 5-7 minutes
Servings: 4

Ingredients
Dressing:
- 1 cup plain Greek yogurt
- 1 tbsp. lemon juice
- 1 tsp. dried dill weed, crushed
- 1 tsp. ground oregano
- 1/2 tsp. salt

Meatballs:
- 1/2 pound (227 g) ground lamb
- 1 tbsp. diced onion
- 1 tsp. dried parsley
- 1 tsp. dried dill weed, crushed
- 1/4 tsp. oregano
- 1/4 tsp. coriander
- 1/4 tsp. ground cumin
- 1/4 tsp. salt
- 4 pita halves Suggested

Toppings:
- red onion
- slivered
- seedless cucumber
- thinly sliced crumbled feta cheese
- sliced black olives
- chopped fresh peppers

Preparation
1. Refrigerate the dressing ingredients while preparing the lamb.
2. In a large mixing bowl, combine all meatball ingredients and whisk to distribute spices.
3. Form the meat mixture into 12 tiny meatballs, spherical or slightly flattened, as desired.
4. Air fried at 390°F for 5 to 7 minutes, or until well cooked. Remove and pat dry with paper towels.
5. To serve, stuff pita pockets with meatballs and your favorite toppings and sprinkle with dressing.

Nutritional information
Calories: 270 Fat: 14 g Protein: 18 g Carbs: 18 g Fiber: 2 g Sugar: 2 g Sodium: 618 mg

Rosemary Lamb Chops

Preparation Time: 30 minutes
Cooking Time: 20 minutes
Servings: 2-3

Ingredients
- 2 tsp. oil
- 1/2 tsp. ground rosemary
- 1/2 tsp. lemon juice
- 1 lb. (454 g) lamb chops, approximately 1-inch thick
- Salt and pepper to taste
- cooking spray

Preparation
1. Rub the lamb chops with the oil, rosemary, and lemon juice mixture. Season with salt and pepper to taste.
2. Allow lamb chops to rest in the fridge for 15 to 20 minutes for the finest taste.
3. Place the lamb chops in the air fryer basket and coat it with nonstick spray.
4. Air fry at 360 °F (182°C) for around 20 minutes,. This will cook the chops to medium-rare. The meat will be moist but no longer pink. For well-done chops, air fry for 1 to 2 minutes longer. Continue cooking for another 12 minutes to achieve rare chops.

Nutritional information
Calories: 237 Fat: 13 g Protein: 30 g Carbs: 0 g Fiber: 0 g Sugar 0 g Sodium: 116 mg

Spicy Lamb Sirloin Steak

Preparation Time: 40 minutes
Cooking Time: 20 minutes
Servings: 4

Ingredients

1 lb. lamb sirloin steaks, pastured, boneless
For the Marinade:
- 1/2 white onion, peeled
- 1 tsp. ground fennel
- 5 garlic cloves, peeled
- 4 slices ginger
- 1 tsp. salt
- 1/2 tsp. ground cardamom
- 1 tsp. garam masala
- 1 tsp. ground cinnamon
- 1 tsp. cayenne pepper

Preparation

1. In a food processor, combine all of the marinade ingredients and pulse until thoroughly combined.
2. Cut the lamb chops with a knife, then place them in a large mixing bowl with the prepared marinade.
3. Refrigerate the lamb chops for at least 30 minutes after thoroughly coating them with the marinade.
4. Then turn on the air fryer, insert the frying basket, coat it with olive oil, close the cover, and warm for 5 minutes at 330°F.
5. Open the fryer, place the lamb chops inside, shut the top, and cook for 15 minutes, or until pleasantly brown and cooked, rotating the steaks halfway through.
6. When the air fryer beeps, remove the lamb steaks to a dish and serve.

Nutritional information

Calories: 182 Carbs: 3 g Fat: 7 g Protein: 24 g Fiber: 1 g

Air Fryer Lamb Chops

Prep time: 5 minutes
cook time: 7 minutes
total time: 12 minutes
4 servings

Ingredients
- 4 lamb chops
- 2 tbsp olive oil
- 1 tbsp minced garlic
- 2 tbsp fresh basil
- 1 tbsp oregano
- ½ tsp ground pepper
- ½ tsp salt
- fresh thyme for garnish

Preparation
1. To begin, combine all ingredients except the fresh thyme in a big Ziplock bag. Shake the bag until the lamb chops are evenly covered in the olive oil and spices.
2. At this stage, either warm the air fryer to 400 degrees Fahrenheit and air fry immediately OR place the Ziplock bag in the refrigerator for up to 24 hours to marinate.
3. After preheating the air fryer, place the lamb chops in the air fryer basket or on the air fryer pan.
4. 7 to 10 minutes in the air fryer. Check the internal temperature of the meat with a meat thermometer after 7 minutes and add further air frying time if necessary.
5. Finally, remove the meat from the air fryer after it has achieved the correct temperature.
6. Allow 5 minutes for the meat to rest before serving and slicing.
7. If desired, garnish with fresh thyme.

Nutritional information
calories: 353kcal, carbohydrates: 2g, protein: 42g, fat: 15g, saturated fat: 6g, polyunsaturated fat: 1g, monounsaturated fat: 10g, cholesterol: 129mg, sodium: 391mg, potassium: 566mg, fiber: 1g, sugar: 1g, vitamin a: 76IU, vitamin c: 1mg, calcium: 46mg, iron: 4mg

Herbed Lamb Chops

Preparation Time: 1 hour 10 minutes
Cooking Time: 13 minutes
Servings: 4

Ingredients

- 1 lb. lamb chops, pastured
- For the Marinate:
- 2 tbsp. lemon juice
- 1 tsp. dried rosemary
- 1 tsp. salt
- 1 tsp. dried thyme 1 tsp. coriander
- 1 tsp. dried oregano
- 2 tbsp. olive oil

Preparation

1. To make the marinade, add all of the ingredients in a mixing bowl and whisk until mixed.
2. Pour the marinade into a large plastic bag, add the lamb chops, close the bag, and flip it upside down to coat the lamb chops with the marinade. Refrigerate for at least 1 hour.
3. Then turn on the air fryer, insert the fryer basket, coat it with olive oil, close the cover, and warm for 5 minutes at 390°F.
4. Open the fryer, place the marinated lamb chops inside, shut the top, and cook for 8 minutes or until pleasantly brown and cooked, turning midway during the frying.
5. When the air fryer sounds, remove the lamb chops to a dish and serve.

Nutritional information

Calories: 177.4 Carbs: 1.7 g Fat: 8 g Protein: 23.4 g Fiber: 0.5 g

Appetizer Recipes

Mini Sweet Pepper Poppers

Prep Time: 15 minutes
Cook Time: 8 minutes
Yields 16 halves (4 per serving)

Ingredients
- 8 mini sweet peppers
- 4 ounces full-fat cream cheese, softened
- 4 slices sugar-free bacon, cooked and crumbled
- 1/4 cup shredded pepper jack cheese

Preparation
1. The peppers' tops should be removed, and they should then be cut in half lengthwise. To remove the membranes and seeds, use a small knife.
2. Combine cream cheese, bacon, and pepper jack in a small bowl.
3. Each sweet pepper should have 3 teaspoons of the mixture inserted, smoothed out. Put the object in the fryer basket.
4. Set the timer for 8 minutes and raise the temperature to 400°F.
5. Serve hot.

Nutritional information
per serving calories: 176 protein: 7.4 g fiber: 0.9 g net carbohydrates: 2.7 g fat: 13.4 g sodium: 309 mg carbohydrates: 3.6 g sugar: 2.2 g

Ranch Roasted Almonds

Prep Time: 5 minutes
Cook Time: 6 minutes
Yields 2 cups (1/4 cup per serving)

Ingredients
- 2 cups raw almonds
- 2 tablespoons unsalted butter, melted
- 1/2 (1-ounce) ranch dressing mix packet

Preparation
1. Almonds should be coated evenly in butter in a big bowl. Almonds are covered with ranch mix; toss. Almonds should be put in the air fryer basket.
2. The timer should be set for 6 minutes with the temperature adjusted to 320°F.
3. During cooking, shake the basket two or three times.
4. Give it at least 20 minutes to cool. Almonds start out soft but get crunchier as they cool. Keep for up to three days in an airtight container.

Nutritional information

per serving calories: 190 protein: 6.0 g fiber: 3.0 g net carbohydrates: 4.0 g fat: 16.7 g sodium: 133 mg carbohydrates: 7.0 g sugar: 1.0 g

Low Carb Lemon Blueberry Muffins (Air Fryer)

Prep Time: 5 minutes
Cook Time: 12 minutes
Total Time: 17 minutes
Serving 6 Muffins

Ingredients

Muffins
- 1 cup almond flour
- 1 teaspoon baking powder
- ¼ teaspoon salt
- ⅓ cup erythritol
- 1 large egg
- 2 tablespoon butter melted and cooled
- ¼ cup whole milk
- 1 teaspoon vanilla extract
- 1 tablespoon lemon juice
- 1 teaspoon lemon zest
- ½ cup blueberries

Streusel Topping
- 1 tablespoon almond flour
- 2 tablespoon erythritol
- 1 tablespoon butter

Preparation

Muffins
1. Preheat air fryer to 300°F.
2. Almond flour, baking soda, and salt should all be combined in a small basin. Place aside.
3. Mix the erythritol, cooled melted butter, and egg in a large basin.
4. Including everything else but the blueberries. Using a rubber spatula, mix everything well.
5. Once they are thoroughly incorporated into the mixture, gently fold in the blueberries.
6. About 1.5 tablespoons of the muffin batter should be scooped into each silicone muffin liner.
7. The muffins should be cooked in the air fryer basket for 10 minutes at 300°F. You might have to complete this in groups.

Sprinkle Topping

8. Combine the ingredients in a small bowl and stir until crumbly.
9. After adding the streusel topping, air fried the muffins for a further 2-4 minutes at 300°F.
10. Muffins should cool in the air fryer basket before being removed to avoid crumbling.

Tips:

Due to their extreme moistness, these muffins might easily crumble. When they are completely cold, take them out of the muffin liners and set them upside-down on a cooling rack to assist the bottoms of the muffins cool.

Every two minutes, rotate the muffins in the air fryer basket (optional).

The essential information to create this recipe is provided on this recipe card. Please read the material above the recipe card if you have any more queries or would want to see modifications.

Nutritional information

Amount per Serving Calories 112 Fat 10g Carbohydrates 4g Fiber 1g Sugar 2g Protein 3g

Mozzarella Pizza Crust

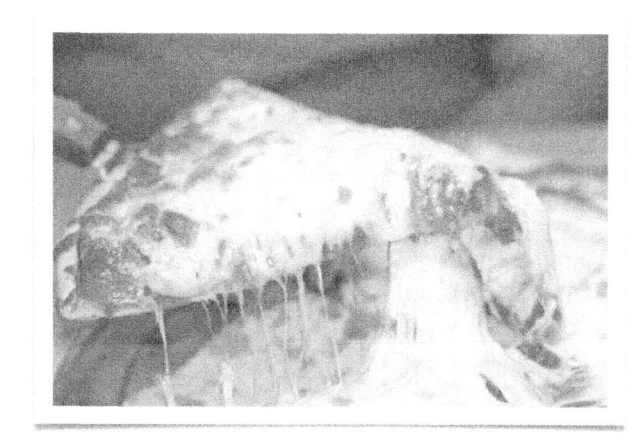

Prep Time: 5 minutes
Cook Time: 10 minutes
Serves 1

Ingredients
- 1/2 cup shredded whole-milk mozzarella cheese
- 2 tablespoons blanched finely ground almond flour
- 1 tablespoon full-fat cream cheese
- 1 large egg white

Preparation
1. In a medium microwave-safe bowl, combine the cream cheese, mozzarella, and almond flour. 30 seconds in the microwave. Stir until a smooth dough ball forms. Stir in the egg white until a soft, round dough forms.
2. Into a 6" spherical pizza crust, press.
3. Place the crust on a piece of parchment that has been cut to fit the air fryer basket and put it in the air fryer.
4. Set the timer for 10 minutes and raise the temperature to 350°F.
5. Serve immediately after flipping after 5 minutes and after adding any desired toppings to the crust at this point.

Nutritional information

per serving calories: 314 protein: 19.9 g fiber: 1.5 g net carbohydrates: 3.6 g fat: 22.7 g sodium: 457 mg carbohydrates: 5.1 g sugar: 1.8 g

Air Fryer Stuffed Mushrooms

Prep: 20 minutes
Cook: 10 minutes
Additional: 5 minutes
Total: 35 minutes
Servings: 6

Ingredient
- 1 (16 ounce) package whole white button mushrooms
- 2 scallions
- 4 ounces cream cheese, softened
- ¼ cup finely shredded sharp Cheddar cheese
- ¼ teaspoon ground paprika
- 1 pinch salt
- cooking spray

Preparation
1. Clean the mushrooms lightly with a moist towel. Remove and discard the stems.
2. Shallots should be minced, with the white and green portions separated.
3. Set an air fryer at 360 degrees Fahrenheit (182 degrees C).
4. In a separate bowl, mix cream cheese, Cheddar cheese, paprika, salt, and the white sections of the scallions. Fill the mushroom cavities with filling by pushing it in with the back of a tiny spoon.
5. Place the mushrooms inside the air fryer basket after spraying it with cooking oil. You might need to cook the food in two batches depending on the size of your air fryer.
6. About 8 minutes into the cooking process, the filling should be gently browned. Continue with the remaining mushrooms.
7. Before serving, sprinkle scallion greens over the mushrooms and allow it cool for five minutes.

Nutritional information
Per serving, there are 104 calories, 5g of protein, 3.5g of carbs, 8.4g of fat, 25.7mg of cholesterol, and 116.3mg of sodium.

Bacon-Wrapped Jalapeño Poppers

Prep Time: 15 minutes
Cook Time: 12 minutes
Serves 4

Ingredients
- 6 jalapeños (about 4" long each)
- 3 ounces full-fat cream cheese
- 1/3 cup shredded medium Cheddar cheese
- 1/4 teaspoon garlic powder
- 12 slices sugar-free bacon

Preparation
1. The jalapenos should have their tops removed before being split lengthwise down the middle. Carefully remove the white membrane and seeds from peppers using a knife.
2. Cream cheese, Cheddar, and garlic powder should be combined in a sizable microwave-safe bowl. Stir after 30 seconds in the microwave. Insert cheese mixture into the jalapenos' hollows.
3. Each jalapeno half should have a slice of bacon wrapped completely around it. Place in the basket of the air fryer.
4. Set the timer for 12 minutes and raise the temperature to 400°F.
5. Halfway through the cooking time, turn the peppers. Serve hot.

Nutritional information
per serving calories: 246 protein: 14.4 g fiber: 0.6 g net carbohydrates: 2.0 g fat: 17.9 g sodium: 625 mg carbohydrates: 2.6 g sugar: 1.6 g

Prosciutto-Wrapped Parmesan Asparagus

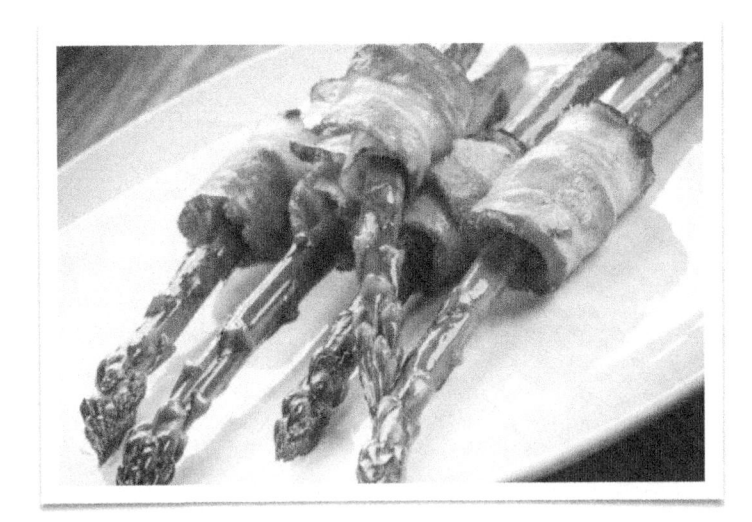

Prep Time: 10 minutes
Cook Time: 10 minutes
Serves 4

Ingredients
- 1 pound asparagus
- 12 (0.5 ounce) slices prosciutto
- 1 tablespoon coconut oil, melted
- 2 teaspoons lemon juice
- 1/8 teaspoon red pepper flakes
- 1/3 cup grated Parmesan cheese
- 2 tablespoons salted butter, melted

Preparation
1. Place a slice of prosciutto and an asparagus spear on a spotless work surface.
2. Lemon juice and coconut oil should be drizzled on. Over the asparagus, smear Parmesan and red pepper flakes. Wrap the spear of asparagus in prosciutto. Place in the basket of the air fryer.
3. Set the timer for 10 minutes and raise the temperature to 375°F.
4. Before serving, drizzle some butter over the asparagus roll.

Nutritional information
per serving calories: 263 protein: 13.9 g fiber: 2.4 g net carbohydrates: 4.3 g fat: 20.2 g sodium: 368 mg carbohydrates: 6.7 g sugar: 2.2 g

Bacon-Wrapped Onion Rings

Prep Time: 5 minutes
Cook Time: 10 minutes
Serves 4

Ingredients
- 1 large onion, peeled
- 1 tablespoon sriracha
- 8 slices sugar-free bacon

Preparation
1. Slice the onion into 1/4"-thick slices, brush with Sriracha, then wrap two slices of onion rings in bacon. Place the onion and bacon rings into the air fryer basket.
2. Set the timer for 10 minutes and raise the temperature to 350°F.
3. Halfway through cooking, flip the onion rings with tongs; when bacon is fully cooked and crispy, serve warm.

Nutritional information
per serving calories: 105 protein: 7.5 g fiber: 0.6 g net carbohydrates: 3.7 g fat: 5.9 g sodium: 401 mg carbohydrates: 4.3 g sugar: 2.3 g

Spicy Spinach Artichoke Dip

Prep Time: 10 minutes
Cook Time: 10 minutes
Serves 6

Ingredients

- 10 ounces frozen spinach, drained and thawed
- 1 (14-ounce) can artichoke hearts, drained and chopped
- 1/4 cup chopped pickled jalapeños
- 8 ounces full-fat cream cheese, softened
- 1/4 cup full-fat mayonnaise
- 1/4 cup full-fat sour cream
- 1/2 teaspoon garlic powder
- 1/4 cup grated Parmesan cheese
- 1 cup shredded pepper jack cheese

Preparation

1. In a 4-cup baking bowl, combine all the ingredients. Place in the basket of the air fryer.
2. The timer should be set for 10 minutes with the temperature adjusted to 320°F.
3. Remove when bubbling and brown. Serve hot.

Nutritional information

per serving calories: 226 protein: 10.0 g fiber: 3.7 g net carbohydrates: 6.5 g fat: 15.9 g sodium: 776 mg carbohydrates: 10.2 g sugar: 3.4 g

Garlic Cheese Bread

Prep Time: 10 minutes
Cook Time: 10 minutes
Serves 2

Ingredients
- 1 cup shredded mozzarella cheese
- 1/4 cup grated Parmesan cheese
- 1 large egg
- 1/2 teaspoon garlic powder

Preparation
1. In a sizable bowl, combine each ingredient. Cut a piece of parchment to fit the basket of your air fryer. Place the mixture in the air fryer basket after shaping it into a circle on the parchment.
2. Set the timer for 10 minutes and raise the temperature to 350°F.
3. Serve hot.

Nutritional information
per serving calories: 258 protein: 19.2 g fiber: 0.1 g net carbohydrates: 3.6 g fat: 16.6 g sodium: 612 mg carbohydrates: 3.7 g sugar: 0.7 g

Beef Jerky

Prep Time: 5 minutes
Cook Time: 4 hours
Serves 10

Ingredients

- 1 pound flat iron beef, thinly sliced
- 1/4 cup soy sauce (or liquid aminos)
- 2 teaspoons Worcestershire sauce
- 1/4 teaspoon crushed red pepper flakes
- 1/4 teaspoon garlic powder
- 1/4 teaspoon onion powder

Preparation

1. All ingredients should be combined and marinated for two hours in the refrigerator in a plastic bag or other covered container.
2. Place every jerky slice in a single layer on the air fryer rack.
3. Set the thermostat to 160 degrees Fahrenheit, and the timer for 4 hours.
4. For up to a week, cool and store in an airtight container.

Nutritional information

per serving calories: 85 protein: 10.2 g fiber: 0.0 g net carbohydrates: 0.6 g fat: 3.5 g sodium: 387 mg carbohydrates: 0.6 g sugar: 0.2 g

Mozzarella-Stuffed Meatballs

Prep Time: 15 minutes
Cook Time: 15 minutes
Yields 16 meatballs (4 per serving)

Ingredients
- 1 pound 80/20 ground beef
- 1/4 cup blanched finely ground almond flour
- 1 teaspoon dried parsley
- 1/2 teaspoon garlic powder
- 1/4 teaspoon onion powder
- 1 large egg
- 3 ounces low-moisture, whole-milk mozzarella, cubed
- 1/2 cup low-carb, no-sugar-added pasta sauce
- 1/4 cup grated Parmesan cheese

Preparation
1. Combine ground beef, almond flour, parsley, garlic powder, onion powder, and egg in a sizable bowl. Mix ingredients thoroughly by folding them in.
2. Use your thumb or a spoon to make an indentation in the centre of each meatball, then place a cube of cheese there and shape the meatball around it.
3. If necessary, add the meatballs to the air fryer in batches.
4. Set the timer for 15 minutes and raise the temperature to 350°F.
5. Meatballs are fully cooked when the internal temperature reaches at least 180°F and the exterior is slightly crispy.
6. When the meatballs are done cooking, place them in the sauce and top with grated Parmesan before serving.

Nutritional information
per serving calories: 447 protein: 29.6 g fiber: 1.8 g net carbohydrates: 3.6 g fat: 29.7 g sodium: 509 mg carbohydrates: 5.4 g sugar: 1.6 g

Spicy Buffalo Chicken Dip

Prep Time: 10 minutes
Cook Time: 10 minutes
Serves 4

Ingredients

- 1 cup cooked, diced chicken breast
- 8 ounces full-fat cream cheese, softened
- 1/2 cup buffalo sauce
- 1/3 cup full-fat ranch dressing
- 1/3 cup chopped pickled jalapeños
- 1 1/2 cups shredded medium Cheddar cheese, divided
- 2 scallions, sliced on the bias

Preparation

1. Put the chicken in a sizable bowl. Ranch dressing, buffalo sauce, and cream cheese should be added. Stir the sauces until they are mostly smooth and well combined. Jalapeons and a cup of Cheddar are folded in.
2. Place the remaining Cheddar on top of the mixture after it has been added to a 4-cup round baking dish. Put the dish in the basket of the air fryer.
3. Set the timer for 10 minutes and raise the temperature to 350°F.
4. The dip will bubble and the top will turn brown when it's finished. Add sliced scallions on top. Serve hot.

Nutritional information

per serving calories: 472 protein: 25.6 g fiber: 0.6 g net carbohydrates: 8.5 g fat: 32.0 g sodium: 1,532 mg carbohydrates: 9.1 g sugar: 7.4 g

Crustless Three-Meat Pizza

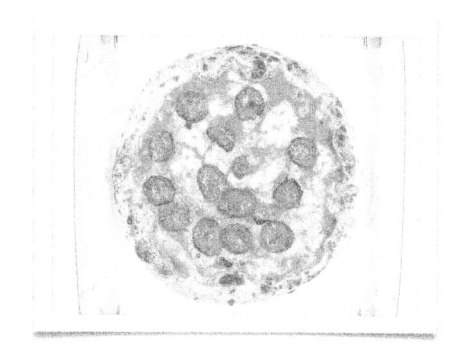

Prep Time: 5 minutes
Cook Time: 5 minutes
Serves 1

Ingredients
- 1/2 cup shredded mozzarella cheese
- 7 slices pepperoni
- 1/4 cup cooked ground sausage
- 2 slices sugar-free bacon, cooked and crumbled
- 1 tablespoon grated Parmesan cheese
- 2 tablespoons low-carb, sugar-free pizza sauce, for dipping

Preparation
1. Put mozzarella on the bottom of a 6" cake pan, add pepperoni, sausage, and bacon, top with Parmesan, and put pan into air fryer basket.
2. Set the thermostat to 400°F, and then set a 5-minute timer.
3. Serve warm with pizza sauce on the side and remove when cheese is bubbling and golden.

Nutritional information
per serving calories: 466 protein: 28.1 g fiber: 0.5 g net carbohydrates: 4.7 g fat: 34.0 g sodium: 1,446 mg carbohydrates: 5.2 g sugar: 1.6 g

Garlic Tomatoes

Preparation Time: 7 minutes
Cooking Time: 15 minutes
Servings: 4

Ingredients
- 3 tbsp. vinegar
- 1/2 tsp. thyme, dried
- 4 tomatoes
- 1 tbsp. olive oil
- Salt and black pepper to taste
- 1 garlic clove, minced

Preparation
1. Preheat your air fryer to 390°F. Scratch the tomatoes into halves and remove the seeds.

Please place them in a big bowl and toss them with oil, salt, pepper, garlic, and thyme.
2. Place them into the air fryer and cook for 15 minutes. Drizzle with vinegar and serve.

Nutritional information

Calories: 28.9 Total Fat: 2.4 g Carbs: 2.0 g Protein: 0.4 g

Side dishes

Roasted Garlic

Prep time: 5 minutes
Cook Time: 20 minutes
Yields 12 cloves (1 per serving)

Ingredients
- 1 medium head garlic
- 2 teaspoons avocado oil

Preparation
1. Garlic should have any hanging peel removed, but the cloves should remain covered. Trim off 1/4 of the garlic head to reveal the cloves' tips.
2. Avocado oil should be drizzled. Put the garlic head entirely inside a small piece of aluminium foil. Put it in the basket of the air fryer.
3. Set the timer for 20 minutes and raise the temperature to 400°F. Check your garlic after 15 minutes if the head is a little smaller.
4. Garlic should be very soft and golden brown when finished.
5. Cloves should easily pop out and can be spread or sliced when ready to serve. For up to five days, keep in the refrigerator in an airtight container. Additionally, you can freeze individual cloves on a baking sheet, then place all of the frozen cloves in a freezer-safe storage bag.

Nutritional information

per serving calories: 11 protein: 0.2 g fiber: 0.1 g net carbohydrates: 0.9 g fat: 0.7 g sodium: 0 mg carbohydrates: 1.0 g sugar: 0.0 g

Veggie Quesadilla

Prep time: 10 minutes
Cook Time: 5 minutes
Serves 2

Ingredients
- 1 tablespoon coconut oil
- 1/2 medium green bell pepper, seeded and chopped
- 1/4 cup diced red onion
- 1/4 cup chopped white mushrooms
- 4 flatbread dough tortillas
- 2/3 cup shredded pepper jack cheese
- 1/2 medium avocado, peeled, pitted, and mashed
- 1/4 cup full-fat sour cream
- 1/4 cup mild salsa

Preparation
1. Warm up the coconut oil in a medium skillet over medium heat. In a skillet, combine the pepper, onion, and mushrooms. Sauté for 3 to 5 minutes, or until the peppers start to soften.
2. On a work surface, arrange two tortillas and top each with half a slice of cheese. Add the remaining cheese, the sautéed vegetables, and the final two tortillas to the top. Carefully place the quesadillas in the air fryer basket.
3. Set the thermostat to 400°F, and then set a 5-minute timer.
4. About halfway through the cooking process, flip the quesadillas. Serve warm with salsa, avocado, and sour cream.

Nutritional information
per serving calories: 795 protein: 34.5 g fiber: 6.5 g net carbohydrates: 12.9 g fat: 61.3 g sodium: 1,051 mg carbohydrates: 19.4 g sugar: 7.4 g

Kale Chips

Prep time: 5 minutes
Cook Time: 5 minutes
Serves 4

Ingredients
- 4 cups stemmed kale
- 2 teaspoons avocado oil
- 1/2 teaspoon salt

Preparation

1. Kale should be mixed with avocado oil and salt in a big bowl. Place in the basket of the air fryer.
2. Set the thermostat to 400°F, and then set a 5-minute timer.
3. When cooked, kale will be crispy. Serve right away.

Nutritional information

per serving calories: 25 protein: 0.5 g fiber: 0.4 g net carbohydrates: 0.7 g fat: 2.2 g sodium: 295 mg carbohydrates: 1.1 g sugar: 0.3 g

Zucchini Parmesan Chips

Prep time: 10 minutes
Cook Time: 10 minutes
Serves 4

Ingredients
- 2 medium zucchini
- 1 ounce pork rinds
- 1/2 cup grated Parmesan cheese
- 1 large egg

Preparation

1. Slices of zucchini should be 1/4" thick. Place for 30 minutes to drain excess moisture between two layers of paper towels or a clean kitchen towel.

2. Pork rinds should be placed in a food processor and pulsed until very fine. Pour into a large bowl, then stir in the Parmesan.
3. In a small bowl, beat the egg.
4. Slices of zucchini should be thoroughly coated after being dipped in egg and then pork rind mixture. Working in batches as necessary, carefully place each slice in a single layer into the air fryer basket.
5. Set the timer for 10 minutes and raise the temperature to 320°F.
6. Midway through the cooking process, flip the chips. Serve hot.

Nutritional information

per serving calories: 121 protein: 9.9 g fiber: 0.6 g net carbohydrates: 3.2 g fat: 6.7 g sodium: 364 mg carbohydrates: 3.8 g sugar: 1.6 g

Fried Pickles

Prep time: 10 minutes
Cook Time: 5 minutes
Serves 4

Ingredients

- 1 tablespoon coconut flour
- 1/3 cup blanched finely ground almond flour
- 1 teaspoon chili powder
- 1/4 teaspoon garlic powder
- 1 large egg
- 1 cup sliced pickles

Preparation

1. In a medium bowl, combine the garlic powder, chilli powder, almond flour, and coconut flour.
2. In a small bowl, whisk the egg.
3. Before dipping each pickle in the egg, pat it dry with a paper towel. After that, coat in the flour mixture. Pickles should be placed in the air fryer basket.
4. Set the thermostat to 400°F, and then set a 5-minute timer.
5. Midway through the cooking process, turn the pickles over.

Nutritional information

per serving calories: 85 protein: 4.3 g fiber: 2.3 g net carbohydrates: 2.3 g fat: 6.1 g sodium: 351 mg carbohydrates: 4.6 g sugar: 1.2 g

Roasted Eggplant

Prep time: 15 minutes
Cook Time: 15 minutes
Serves 4

Ingredients
- 1 large eggplant
- 2 tablespoons olive oil
- 1/4 teaspoon salt
- 1/2 teaspoon garlic powder

Preparation
1. Remove the eggplant's top and bottom. Round slices of eggplant should be 1/4" thick.
2. Apply olive oil to the slices. Add salt and garlic powder to taste. Put the air fryer basket with the eggplant slices inside.
3. Set the timer for 15 minutes and raise the temperature to 390°F.
4. Serve right away.

Nutritional information
per serving calories: 91 protein: 1.3 g fiber: 3.7 g net carbohydrates: 3.8 g fat: 6.7 g sodium: 147 mg carbohydrates: 7.5 g sugar: 4.4 g

Avocado Fries

Prep time: 15 minutes
Cook Time: 5 minutes
Serves 4

Ingredients
- 2 medium avocados
- 1 ounce pork rinds, finely ground

Preparation
1. Each avocado is divided in half. Eliminate the pit. Peel the fruit carefully, then cut it into 1/4"-thick slices of flesh.

2. In a medium bowl, add the pork rinds and press each avocado slice into the pork rinds to evenly coat them. Put the pieces of avocado in the air fryer basket.
3. Set the timer for 5 minutes and raise the temperature to 350°F.
4. Serve right away.

Nutritional information

per serving calories: 153 protein: 5.4 g fiber: 4.6 g net carbohydrates: 1.3 g fat: 11.9 g sodium: 121 mg carbohydrates: 5.9 g sugar: 0.2 g

Coconut Flour Cheesy Garlic Biscuits

Prep time: 10 minutes
Cook Time: 12 minutes
Serves 4

Ingredients
- 1/3 cup coconut flour
- 1/2 teaspoon baking powder
- 1/2 teaspoon garlic powder
- 1 large egg
- 1/4 cup unsalted butter, melted and divided
- 1/2 cup shredded sharp Cheddar cheese
- 1 scallion, sliced

Preparation
1. Combine coconut flour, baking soda, and garlic powder in a sizable bowl.
2. Add the egg, scallions, Cheddar cheese, and half of the melted butter after stirring. In a 6" round baking pan, pour the mixture. Place in the basket of the air fryer.
3. The timer should be set for 12 minutes with the temperature adjusted to 320°F.
4. Remove from pan and let cool completely before serving. Divide into four pieces, then top with the remaining melted butter.

Nutritional information

per serving calories: 218 protein: 7.2 g fiber: 3.4 g net carbohydrates: 3.4 g fat: 16.9 g sodium: 177 mg carbohydrates: 6.8 g sugar: 2.1 g

Cilantro Lime Roasted Cauliflower

Prep time: 10 minutes
Cook Time: 7 minutes
Serves 4

Ingredients

- 2 cups chopped cauliflower florets
- 2 tablespoons coconut oil, melted
- 2 teaspoons chili powder
- 1/2 teaspoon garlic powder
- 1 medium lime
- 2 tablespoons chopped cilantro

Preparation

1. Cauliflower should be mixed with coconut oil in a big bowl. Garlic and chilli powder should be added. Put the air fryer basket with the seasoned cauliflower inside.
2. Set the timer for 7 minutes and raise the temperature to 350°F.
3. The cauliflower will be tender and its edges will start to turn golden. Add to the serving bowl.
4. Squeeze the lime's juice over the cauliflower after cutting it into quarters. cilantro is a good garnish.

Nutritional information

per serving calories: 73 protein: 1.1 g fiber: 1.1 g net carbohydrates: 2.2 g fat: 6.5 g sodium: 16 mg carbohydrates: 3.3 g sugar: 1.1 g

Desserts

Coconut Flour Mug Cake

Prep time: 5 minutes
Cook Time: 25 minutes
Serves 1

Ingredients
- 1 large egg
- 2 tablespoons coconut flour
- 2 tablespoons heavy whipping cream
- 2 tablespoons granular erythritol
- 1/4 teaspoon vanilla extract
- 1/4 teaspoon baking powder

Preparation
1. Whisk the egg in a 4-ounce ramekin before adding the other ingredients. until smooth, stir. Place in the basket of the air fryer.
2. Set the timer for 25 minutes and raise the temperature to 300°F. A toothpick should come out clean after completion. Use a spoon to eat straight out of the ramekin. Serve hot.

Nutritional information
per serving calories: 237 protein: 9.9 g fiber: 5.0 g net carbohydrates: 5.7 g sugar alcohol: 30.0 g fat: 16.4 g sodium: 213 mg carbohydrates: 40.7 g sugar: 4.2 g

Almond Butter Cookie Balls

Prep time: 5 minutes
Cook Time: 10 minutes
Yields 10 balls (1 ball per serving)

Ingredients
- 1 cup almond butter
- 1 large egg
- 1 teaspoon vanilla extract
- 1/4 cup low-carb protein powder
- 1/4 cup powdered erythritol
- 1/4 cup shredded unsweetened coconut
- 1/4 cup low-carb, sugar-free chocolate chips
- 1/2 teaspoon ground cinnamon

Preparation
1. Mix almond butter and egg in a big bowl. Vanilla, protein powder, and erythritol should be added.
2. Add cinnamon, chocolate chips, and coconut by folding. Roll into balls. Put the balls in a round 6" baking pan inside the air fryer basket.
3. The timer should be set for 10 minutes with the temperature adjusted to 320°F.
4. Allow to completely cool. Keep in the refrigerator for up to four days in an airtight container.

Nutritional information
per serving calories: 224 protein: 11.2 g fiber: 3.6 g net carbohydrates: 1.3 g sugar alcohol: 10.0 g fat: 16.0 g sodium: 40 mg carbohydrates: 14.9 g sugar: 1.3 g

Vanilla Pound Cake

Prep time: 10 minutes
Cook Time: 25 minutes
Serves 6

Ingredients

- 1 cup blanched finely ground almond flour
- 1/4 cup salted butter, melted
- 1/2 cup granular erythritol
- 1 teaspoon vanilla extract
- 1 teaspoon baking powder
- 1/2 cup full-fat sour cream
- 1 ounce full-fat cream cheese, softened
- 2 large eggs

Preparation

1. Combine almond flour, butter, and erythritol in a sizable bowl.
2. Mix thoroughly after adding the vanilla, baking powder, sour cream, and cream cheese. Add eggs, then blend.
3. Pour the batter in a 6" round baking pan. Put the pan in the air fryer basket.
4. Set the timer for 25 minutes and raise the temperature to 300°F.
5. A toothpick inserted in the centre of the cake will come out clean when it is finished. It shouldn't feel damp in the centre. The cake will crumble if you move it before it has completely cooled.

Nutritional information

per serving calories: 253 protein: 6.9 g fiber: 2.0 g net carbohydrates: 3.2 g sugar alcohol: 20.0 g fat: 22.6 g sodium: 191 mg carbohydrates: 25.2 g sugar: 1.5 g

Pecan Brownies

Prep time: 10 minutes
Cook Time: 20 minutes
Serves 6

Ingredients
- 1/2 cup blanched finely ground almond flour
- 1/2 cup powdered erythritol
- 2 tablespoons unsweetened cocoa powder
- 1/2 teaspoon baking powder
- 1/4 cup unsalted butter, softened
- 1 large egg
- 1/4 cup chopped pecans
- 1/4 cup low-carb, sugar-free chocolate chips

Preparation
1. Combine almond flour, erythritol, cocoa powder, and baking powder in a sizable bowl. Add butter and egg and stir.
2. Add chocolate chips and pecans by folding. Into a 6" round baking pan, scoop the mixture. In the air fryer basket, put the pan.
3. Set the timer for 20 minutes and raise the temperature to 300°F.
4. A toothpick inserted in the middle will come out clean when the food is fully cooked. Give the food 20 minutes to completely cool and set.

Nutritional information

per serving calories: 215 protein: 4.2 g fiber: 2.8 g net carbohydrates: 2.3 g sugar alcohol: 16.7 g fat: 18.9 g sodium: 53 mg carbohydrates: 21.8 g sugar: 0.6 g

Blackberry Crisp

Prep time: 5 minutes
Cook Time: 15 minutes
Serves 4

Ingredients
- 2 cups blackberries
- 1/3 cup powdered erythritol
- 2 tablespoons lemon juice
- 1/4 teaspoon xanthan gum
- 1 cup Crunchy Granola

Preparation
1. Blackberries, erythritol, lemon juice, and xanthan gum are combined in a big bowl.
2. Pour the mixture into a 6" round baking dish, then foil it. Place in the basket of the air fryer.
3. Set the timer for 12 minutes and raise the temperature to 350°F.
4. Remove the foil and stir when the timer sounds.
5. Add granola on top of the mixture before placing it back in the air fryer basket.
6. Set the oven to 320°F, and cook the top for 3 minutes, or until golden.
7. Serve hot.

Nutritional information
per serving calories: 496 protein: 9.2 g fiber: 12.5 g net carbohydrates: 9.7 g sugar alcohol: 21.8 g fat: 42.1 g sodium: 5 mg carbohydrates: 44.0 g sugar: 5.7 g

Pumpkin Spice Pecans

Prep time: 5 minutes
Cook Time: 6 minutes
Serves 4

Ingredients
- 1 cup whole pecans
- 1/4 cup granular erythritol
- 1 large egg white
- 1/2 teaspoon ground cinnamon
- 1/2 teaspoon pumpkin pie spice
- 1/2 teaspoon vanilla extract

Preparation

1. In a big bowl, mix everything together until the pecans are well-coated. Place in the basket of the air fryer.
2. Set the timer for 6 minutes and raise the temperature to 300°F.
3. Cooking requires two to three tosses.
4. Allow to completely cool. Keep for up to three days in an airtight container.

Nutritional information
per serving calories: 178 protein: 3.2 g fiber: 2.6 g net carbohydrates: 1.4 g sugar alcohol: 15.0 g fat: 17.0 g sodium: 13 mg carbohydrates: 19.0 g sugar: 1.1 g

Toasted Coconut Flakes

Prep time: 5 minutes
Cook Time: 3 minutes
Serves 4

Ingredients
- 1 cup unsweetened coconut flakes
- 2 teaspoons coconut oil
- 1/4 cup granular erythritol
- 1/8 teaspoon salt

Preparation

1. In a big bowl, combine oil and coconut flakes and toss to combine. Salt and erythritol should be added.

2. Coconut flakes should be added to the air fryer basket.
3. Set the thermostat to 300°F and start a 3-minute timer.
4. When one minute has passed, toss the flakes. If you prefer more golden coconut flakes, add another minute.
5. Keep for up to three days in an airtight container.

Nutritional information
per serving calories: 165 protein: 1.3 g fiber: 2.7 g net carbohydrates: 2.6 g sugar alcohol: 15.0 g fat: 15.5 g sodium: 76 mg carbohydrates: 20.3 g sugar: 0.5 g

Pan Peanut Butter Cookies

Prep time: 5 minutes
Cook Time: 8 minutes
Serves 8

Ingredients
- 1 cup no-sugar-added smooth peanut butter
- 1/3 cup granular erythritol
- 1 large egg
- 1 teaspoon vanilla extract

Preparation
1. Blend all the ingredients in a sizable bowl. The mixture will start to thicken after two more minutes of stirring.
2. Eight discs of the mixture should be formed by rolling it into balls and gently pressing down.
3. Cut a piece of parchment to size to fit your air fryer and put it in the basket. Arrange the cookies on the parchment, working in batches as needed.
4. The timer should be set for 8 minutes with the temperature adjusted to 320°F.
5. At the six-minute point, turn the cookies. Serve after having fully cooled.

Nutritional information
per serving calories: 210 protein: 8.8 g fiber: 2.0 g net carbohydrates: 2.1 g sugar alcohol: 10.0 g fat: 17.5 g sodium: 8 mg carbohydrates: 14.1 g sugar: 1.1 g

Mini Cheesecake

Prep time: 10 minutes
Cook Time: 15 minutes
Serves 2

Ingredients
- 1/2 cup walnuts
- 2 tablespoons salted butter
- 2 tablespoons granular erythritol
- 4 ounces full-fat cream cheese, softened
- 1 large egg
- 1/2 teaspoon vanilla extract
- 1/8 cup powdered erythritol

Preparation
1. Put butter, walnuts, and erythritol granules in a food processor. To form dough, pulse the ingredients until they bind together.
2. Put the dough-filled 4" springform pan into the air fryer basket.
3. Set the thermostat to 400°F, and then set a 5-minute timer.
4. Remove the crust and let it cool when the timer goes off.
5. Cream cheese, egg, vanilla extract, and erythritol powder should be thoroughly combined in a medium bowl.
6. Spread the mixture over the baked walnut crust before putting it in the air fryer basket.
7. Set the timer for 10 minutes and raise the temperature to 300°F.
8. After finishing, let it chill for two hours before serving.

Nutritional information
per serving calories: 531 protein: 11.4 g fiber: 2.3 g net carbohydrates: 5.1 g sugar alcohol: 24.0 g fat: 48.3 g sodium: 333 mg carbohydrates: 31.4 g sugar: 2.9 g

Made in the USA
Monee, IL
16 November 2022